THE LEADER'S DEVOTIONAL

THE LEADER'S DEVOTIONAL

90 DAYS OF BIBLICAL WISDOM
FOR HONORING GOD IN ALL YOU DO

DAVID GREEN WITH BILL HIGH

BakerBooks

a division of Baker Publishing Group
Grand Rapids, Michigan

© 2024 by Hobby Lobby Stores, Inc., and Generational Legacy Counsel, LLC

Published by Baker Books
a division of Baker Publishing Group
Grand Rapids, Michigan
BakerBooks.com

Printed in China

Library of Congress Cataloging-in-Publication Data
Names: Green, David, 1941 November 13– author. | High, Bill, author.
Title: The leader's devotional : 90 days of biblical wisdom for honoring God in all you do / David Green with Bill High.
Description: Grand Rapids, Michigan : Baker Books, a division of Baker Publishing Group, [2024] | Includes bibliographical references.
Identifiers: LCCN 2024004274 | ISBN 9781540903990 (cloth) | ISBN 9781493445790 (ebook)
Subjects: LCSH: Christianity—Prayers and devotions. | Leadership.
Classification: LCC BV245 .G654 2024 | DDC 242/.2—dc23/eng/20240304
LC record available at https://lccn.loc.gov/2024004274

Unless otherwise indicated, Scripture quotations are from the Holy Bible, New International Version®, NIV®. Copyright © 1973, 1978, 1984, 2011 by Biblica, Inc.® Used by permission of Zondervan. All rights reserved worldwide. www.zondervan.com. The "NIV" and "New International Version" are trademarks registered in the United States Patent and Trademark Office by Biblica, Inc.®

Scripture quotations labeled ESV are from The Holy Bible, English Standard Version® (ESV®). Copyright © 2001 by Crossway, a publishing ministry of Good News Publishers. Used by permission. All rights reserved. ESV Text Edition: 2016

Scripture quotations labeled NASB are from the (NASB®) New American Standard Bible®. Copyright © 1960, 1971, 1977, 1995, 2020 by The Lockman Foundation. Used by permission. All rights reserved. www.lockman.org

Some content in this book has been adapted from David Green with Bill High, *Leadership Not by the Book: 12 Unconventional Principles to Drive Incredible Results* (Grand Rapids: Baker Books, 2022).

Some names and identifying details have been changed to protect the privacy of individuals.

Cover design by Laura Powell

The authors are represented by the literary agency of A Drop of Ink, LLC.

Baker Publishing Group publications use paper produced from sustainable forestry practices and postconsumer waste whenever possible.

24 25 26 27 28 29 30   7 6 5 4 3 2 1

And David shepherded them with integrity of heart;

with skillful hands he led them.

Psalm 78:72

Which Book Are You Reading?

> All Scripture is God-breathed and is useful for teaching, rebuking, correcting and training in righteousness, so that the servant of God may be thoroughly equipped for every good work.
>
> 2 Timothy 3:16–17

I've been interviewed a few times by reporters from *Fox Business News* and other news outlets over the years. Many of these hardworking people went to college to study business or finance, and they read the *Wall Street Journal*. There are many excellent business principles and best practices you can learn from these colleges and publications. You could say this kind of approach is business "by the book."

I'm grateful for these kinds of resources. I'm also forever grateful that God gave us another book: the Bible. God's book offers so much more than anything the wisdom of this world can give us. Just a few characteristics of God's book are:

- It's eternal—God's Word will last forever.
- It's breathed (inspired) by God—the Creator of life has given us His manual for life.
- It's practically useful—God's Word will teach us the right way to go, direct us away from wrong paths, and equip us to live out what God created us to become and do.

I'm constantly amazed at how the Bible speaks practically to me about issues like how to treat vendors, how to govern the company, or how to lead our family. There are great guidelines on what to look for in senior leadership or the right ways to treat customers. The list can go on and on. It's not simply a book to read on Sunday or simply an inspirational book. It can help me make decisions on billion-dollar questions about the future of Hobby Lobby and daily decisions like how many scissors to carry. The Psalms promise that God's Word is a lamp for our feet and a light for our path—in every domain of life (Ps. 119:105).

So, which book are you reading these days? Are you living your life and running your business more "by the book" or more "by *the* Book"?

How are you interacting with the Bible right now? What is one small step you could take this week to create more time and space to engage with God's Word?

Not by the Book?

Do not conform to the pattern of this world, but be transformed by the renewing of your mind.

Romans 12:2

I sometimes wrestle with big questions like whether we should price our candy melts for $2.99 or $1.99. Some would laugh at decisions like that and just call it a business decision. But I see all decisions as spiritual decisions.

You see, it really makes a big difference. That one item—when you have one thousand stores—may lead to a million more packages that get sold. That leads to more profit and ultimately more money that we get to give away to reach more people for Christ.

There's no formula that leads us to the absolute right decisions. I sometimes joke with our people that we do a lot of wrong things and we do a lot of right things—the trouble is we don't know which is which.

But I do know this—if our leadership follows a book, system, or pattern, then we're probably not where we are supposed to be.

Why do I say that? It seems that God's way is never straight down the highway. He's always got a different plan.

That's why Gideon went into battle with three hundred men, not ten thousand.

That's why Jericho was taken with a seven-day march around the city and the blast of a trumpet.

That's why Paul and Silas didn't flee the prison even when an earthquake opened the doors.

That's why David fought a battle with a giant with a sling and a stone.

That's why Elijah poured water on the sacrifice when he was supposed to light a fire.

I love the Scripture that says, "Your path led through the sea, your way through the mighty waters, though your footprints were not seen" (Ps. 77:19).

What's the most unconventional decision you've made in leading your organization, your family, or your life? How did it turn out? Are there ways that you are leading your organization or your family that are conforming to the world and need to change?

Find Your Whatever

Whatever your hand finds to do, do it with all your might.

Ecclesiastes 9:10

I had a person come join our company who was immensely talented. After a short time, his work seemed to suffer and the original energy he displayed wore off. He told us that he didn't think the role was a good fit. So we put him in another role. The same thing happened. His enthusiasm soon went down and so did his work.

This happened a few times, and he always said the same thing: "I just wasn't passionate about the job."

Unfortunately, I hear stories like this from other leaders too. We have people who work for us who don't seem motivated; they don't seem to work with purpose or passion.

What's the right solution? The right job, or the right attitude?

We all have jobs or tasks in our lives that we'd just as soon not do—or we avoid all together. But if we approach them half-heartedly or without energy, passion, and purpose, we'll never achieve all God has for us.

I remember one of my first jobs was fetching tools for an electrician. But when I started doing the job, I noticed that the electrician's shop was a mess.

So I organized his shop without anyone asking me. The electrician and his wife were stunned. It was a menial job, but I learned to dig in and work heartily. I truly believe that job was one of my first steps to where I am today.

I sometimes say that you may have a job flipping hamburgers, and if you work half-heartedly, you'll probably not be flipping hamburgers very long. But if you become the best hamburger flipper you can possibly be, then there's no telling what God can do with you.

Long before David became a king, he was a shepherd boy. Imagine what would have happened if he'd been a half-hearted shepherd boy.

———

What do you believe—do we need to find people the right job or the right attitude? Are there any areas of your life where you are less than wholehearted? How can you apply wholeheartedness to that area?

The Secret Sauce

> Therefore everyone who hears these words of mine and puts them into practice is like a wise man who built his house on the rock.
>
> Matthew 7:24

I've had many people ask me, "What is the secret of Hobby Lobby's success?" In the early days I may have answered that question a few different ways, but in recent years I know exactly what to say: *If you boil down the secret sauce to one key ingredient, you will find the one element that makes the others work—listening to God and obeying His Word.*

It all starts with listening to God. Are you making time to really listen to what God is saying? God has spoken to me through reading His Word, through Bible teachers, through my wife, Barbara, and our children, and through circumstances. And on rare occasions God speaks directly to my mind and heart with unmistakable clarity.

God may speak to you in different ways, but the important thing is that God speaks. And when He speaks, the message will always agree with how He has already spoken to us in His

Word—because He isn't a God of confusion. So, if you want to hear what God is saying to you, start by reading the Bible every day, before opening your email.

But Jesus takes it a step further in Matthew 7 when He says it's not enough to hear what God is saying. Unless we put it into practice, we are still foolish people building our lives on sinking sand.

What does it look like to put God's Word into practice? Often I find myself doing one or more of the following:

- **CONFESSING.** To confess means to agree with God about whatever He is saying.
- **REPENTING.** To repent means to change our mind and direction, to turn around. Because we trust God's Word more than our wisdom, we do a 180 and go God's way.
- **TAKING ACTION.** God tells us to love, and love is more than a warm emotion; it's an action. Unless our love for God and people compels us to act, we are only fooling ourselves.

———

Are you in a habit of reading God's Word? If not, what would be a good step for you to take this week? Has God spoken to you about something you haven't put into practice yet? If so, what's holding you back?

13

God's Foolish Wisdom

Do not deceive yourselves. If any of you think you are wise by the standards of this age, you should become "fools" so that you may become wise. For the wisdom of this world is foolishness in God's sight.

1 Corinthians 3:18–19

My family and I have been called fools (and much worse) by several people who subscribe to and want to enforce the "standards of this age." In 1 Corinthians 3 Paul makes two things crystal clear: If you live by God's wisdom as revealed in His Word, you will be considered a fool by many. If, however, you recognize the emptiness and foolishness of this world's wisdom, you can truly become wise.

We see here how God's kingdom turns upside down the conventional wisdom of the prevailing culture.

- The world system says, "Maximize profit to enrich yourself at the expense of others." God's wisdom says, "Maximize so that you can give more to bless others."

- The world system says, "Work seven days a week and squeeze every ounce of productivity out of your employees." God's wisdom says, "Take a full day off each week and encourage your employees to rest and make space for God and community."

- The world system says, "Leaders get to call the shots and tell their subordinates what to do." God's wisdom says, "Leaders are servants who lead by example and sacrifice themselves for the good of their people."

When the world applauds you, beware. Don't take its praise to heart. Stay humble and remember that you live and work for an audience of One. The day will come when each of us will stand before the Lord to give an account for how we stewarded our lives and opportunities. And I know that you, like me, want to hear, "Well done, my good and faithful servant."

I can accept the world calling me a fool if God says, "Well done." How about you?

———

How are you seeking God's wisdom these days? Have you identified wise mentors and spiritual guides who can help you navigate life and work? In what way do you need to accept the label of "fool" to become "wise"?

Three Big-Picture Practices

> Jesus replied: "'Love the Lord your God with all your heart and with all your soul and with all your mind.' This is the first and greatest commandment. And the second is like it: 'Love your neighbor as yourself.'"
>
> Matthew 22:37–39

When writing *Leadership Not by the Book*, I stepped back to reflect on the big picture of my life. From the vantage point of the past fifty years, I noticed three important practices that kept me on (or returned me to) the right path.

1. God-focused practices
2. People-centered practices
3. Commonsense practices

When Jesus was asked in Matthew 22 what the greatest commandment was, He answered simply: love God with everything you have and everything you are. But Jesus didn't stop there; He also said the next most important commandment is to love your neighbor as yourself.

Jesus's admonition to love God and neighbor are the heart and soul of the first two practices. We love God (our God-focused practices) by listening to Him, talking to Him, doing what He says, and following where He leads. Our life, our family, and our business are built on and through our love for God. There is nothing more important.

Our people-centered practices all boil down to loving people well—even people we don't know or like. Recall that when Jesus was asked to define our "neighbor," He told the story of the Good Samaritan; it's the story of how love does the right thing no matter what society says.

Our commonsense practices are what ground us in the real world. We need practical wisdom to run our homes, our ministries, and our companies. We won't find a Bible passage that tells us how many picture frames to order for next season, but we can distill principles from God's Word, our own experiences, and the input of others to make wise decisions.

As you think about these three big-picture practices, which one(s) feel like a strength to you right now? Which one(s), if any, feel like a stretch? Where would you like to focus more attention this week?

Practicing for Heaven

My command is this: Love each other as I have loved you. Greater love has no one than this: to lay down one's life for one's friends.

John 15:12–13

I received a card on my eightieth birthday from one of our employees that read, "I'm a different person today because I watched you serve the Lord." I couldn't have asked for a better gift!

As Christians, our relationships with one another stretch beyond this lifetime. We will be with God and with each other in the new heaven and new earth, forever.

No wonder Jesus emphasized over and over again (as did His apostles) the command to love one another. In John 15, Jesus told His disciples to love each other as He loved them. And how did Jesus demonstrate love? He laid down His life for them, and for all of us.

Of course, like siblings in the back seat of a station wagon on a long drive, we are going to argue and fight, even as Christians. We will offend and take offense. We will need to forgive and repair damaged relationships. Learning to love like Jesus loves will be a lifelong pursuit. So, rather than worrying about perfection, let's focus on progress.

How do you get better at loving people? By practicing loving people! There are no doubt many ways you already love people naturally and authentically. But there are probably a few areas in which you struggle to show love. Where do you need to practice?

How would you describe the health of your love quotient?

- Do you rejoice with those who rejoice and weep with those who weep?
- Do you forgive?
- Do you speak the truth in love, even if the other person may not appreciate it at the time?
- Do you speak directly to someone who's offended you, or do you gossip?
- Do you pray for the needs of people?
- Do you go out of your way to encourage and edify?

We are going to spend a lot of time together in eternity! It would be a good idea to start practicing for heaven now. And if we do, others will want to join us.

Which expression of love do you want to begin practicing more intentionally? What could you do to grow in this area? Who could help you move forward?

Two Things That Last

Your word, LORD, is eternal; it stands firm in the heavens. . . . I will never forget your precepts, for by them you have preserved my life.

Psalm 119:89, 93

There are only two things in life today that will last forever: God's Word and the souls of people. If that's true, what difference should it really make in our day-to-day lives?

Let's focus for a moment on God's Word. Most Christians would agree that we should engage with the Bible by reading it, listening to good teaching based on it, memorizing passages, meditating on its truths, and doing our very best to trust and obey what it says. It is, after all, God's manual for life.

As we invest time in God's Word for our lives, it produces fruit that stands firm. Psalm 1:3 says the person who invests in God's Word is like a tree planted by streams of water. And trees planted by streams of water have deep roots.

But it doesn't stop there. As we grow deep in God's Word, Psalm 1:3 says, we'll also yield fruit. What is that fruit? It's the fruit of the Spirit: love, joy, peace, patience, kindness, goodness, faithfulness, gentleness, and self-control (Gal. 5:22–23).

That fruit makes us attractive to others. Second Corinthians 2:15 says that we are a pleasing aroma to those who are being saved and to those who are perishing.

That pleasing aroma can be part of the first step of seeing others respond in faith to the good news of Jesus Christ. As people respond to that good news, we bear fruit: the fruit of people's souls—the second thing that lasts forever.

I think we get so caught up in the day-to-day of this vaporous life—the daily decisions around life, relationships, and business—that we forget about the long tomorrow. We forget that one day in heaven we'll have the opportunity to be reunited with all people who share our faith. I think those conversations will be so incredible. I get motivated by thinking about all those souls who might come up and say, "Thank you for being willing to share the gospel."

So, what would it look like to receive the eternal Word of God into your heart and mind every day to strengthen and grow your forever soul? How about taking God's Word and planting it in the souls of people who don't know Him yet? In this life we have the opportunity to start practicing for heaven. What are we doing with it?

What is your habit of reading God's Word? Do you have a personal relationship with God's Word yet, or do you only access God's written revelation through others? How can you become more intentional about knowing the Bible and sharing it with others?

Crisis Leadership 101

The LORD will keep you from all harm—he will watch over your life; the LORD will watch over your coming and going both now and forevermore.

Psalm 121:7–8

When the 2020 global pandemic shut down our stores, we found ourselves in a crisis unlike anything we'd ever faced. The rent alone for our stores was $40 million a month, not to mention payroll. What were we to do?

We did the one thing we knew to do: we prayed. Barbara and I literally got on our knees morning, noon, and night asking God for direction, protection, and provision. God began answering those prayers when He spoke powerfully to Barbara, saying: *I will* guide *you through this storm, I will* guard *you as you travel to places never seen before, and, as a result of this experience, I will* groom *you to be better than you could have ever thought possible before now.*

First, God promised to *guide* us. In Psalm 121, God promises to keep His children from harm. God was with us, and if we listened to Him and tried our best to do as He says, He would

22

watch over our coming and going. We could rest in that. We walked by faith, not by sight.

Second, God promised to *guard* us. Not only did our family and our fifty thousand employees need God's protection from COVID-19 but we also needed protection from stress and financial hardship. Jesus came to give His followers abundant life, but all of that was threatened. We needed God's protection.

Third, God promised to *groom* us. I'll be honest, the realities of God guiding and guarding feel good, but God's grooming was and is really hard. The Bible says God disciplines all His children. God's discipline shapes our character, purifies and deepens our faith, and removes unhealthy distractions from our lives. He grooms us to mature us, but no child enjoys being disciplined at the time.

In what situation in your life today do you tend to lose sight of God's guarding presence being with you every moment? What can you do to remind yourself and more fully recognize and rely on God in that situation? How may God be using this challenge to groom you?

God Exalts the Humble

Humble yourselves, therefore, under God's mighty hand, that he may lift you up in due time. Cast all your anxiety on him because he cares for you.

1 Peter 5:6–7

During the 1985 oil market crash, we found ourselves in deep trouble. After fifteen years of consistent growth, I'd become overconfident, and we took on too much long-term debt. When the banks threatened foreclosure, I found myself under my desk every day on my knees, begging God to help us.

I'd grown proud. I thought I had the Midas touch. I was wrong. In my spirit I heard God say to me, *If you're so big, I'm going to let you have it by yourself.*

While I still had life and breath, I was trying to operate the business without the blessing and favor of God. God humbled me and showed me that I wasn't smart enough to lead our business to success on my own.

Yes, I'd learned a lot about how to successfully run a company by then, but did I have enough wisdom to make the best possible decisions literally thousands of times each year? No, not by a long shot. I realized that running a business was a sacred work, just the same as any church or ministry.

So, one of the things I got clarity on while under my desk during that anxious time was this: God is big and I am small. I learned, once again, to humble myself under God's mighty hand. I also learned to give God all of the things that created anxiety (and there were a lot of them) and recognized that He cared for me as a good Father.

Did $50 million suddenly appear in our bank account? No. I kept praying and doing my best to steward what God had given us, and by the end of 1986 we were profitable once more. God lifted me (and Hobby Lobby) up, but first He had to destroy my pride.

Can you think of a time when you were humbled by a setback or failure? What did you learn about God? What did you learn about yourself? Rather than waiting to be humbled, we can choose to humble ourselves before God. What might that look like for you this week?

The Blessings of Stewardship

> This is how one should regard us, as servants of Christ and stewards of the mysteries of God. Moreover, it is required of stewards that they be found faithful.
>
> 1 Corinthians 4:1–2 ESV

At the end of the day, what do we really own? Psalm 24:1 says, "The earth is the LORD's, and everything in it, the world, and all who live in it." God created everything, so He owns it all. Everything.

If God is the owner, then what is my role? I'm a steward—a manager. I manage the resources God puts in my hand. Take it from someone who learned this the hard way: it is much better to be a steward than an owner.

What do I mean?

If you are an owner—of a company, a ministry, a car, whatever it is—the ownership creates an expectation. I'm entitled to drive the car I own, for instance. But if God owns the company and I'm a steward of that company, then I owe the company to do my very best job in taking care of it.

If I own the company, I expect to get paid. I expect to benefit from its profits and to benefit from the proceeds if I sell it. But then I face the question of what to do with that wealth. Do I just pass it on to my children? So many families have been ruined by simply passing financial wealth down to the next generation.

But if I'm a steward of the company, the only question I face is how God would want me to use the wealth. Wealth becomes a tool and not a right. If I own the company, everyone can look to me to make all the important decisions because it is *mine*. But if I'm a steward, everyone participates. The goal is to make the best decisions for the good of the company, not just for me.

When I recognized that God owned Hobby Lobby, a tremendous weight was removed from me. I could make decisions for the good of what I was stewarding. I wonder if a good approach would be to consider changing the title "Chief Executive Officer" to "Chief Steward."

What problems have you witnessed in other leaders who operate as if they own their companies? What do you most want to hand down to your children and grandchildren? How can wealth be a tool for them instead of a curse?

DAY 12

Praying 24/7

Rejoice always, pray continually, give thanks in all circumstances; for this is God's will for you in Christ Jesus.

1 Thessalonians 5:16–18

The foundation of our business is Barbara's prayer life. She often asks God to wake her up in the middle of the night to pray and write in her journal. There would be no Hobby Lobby without Barbara and her commitment to continual prayer.

Many Christians pray before a meal or in church, and those are wonderful examples of prayer. But how might you move from occasional prayer to continual prayer?

The passage above says to "pray continually." Some versions translate it as "pray without ceasing." When I think about praying continually, it helps me to visualize that Jesus is always with me, every single moment of the day. I can begin the day with gratitude, asking myself, *What is something good in my life that I can rejoice over?*

Are you in good health? Did you wake up this morning and get out of bed unassisted? Do your spouse and your children love the Lord? Has God blessed your business? Has God provided you with enough to be generous? If you answered yes to any of the above—rejoice!

We can also treat the day as an ongoing prayer, even as we go off to work. It may be a decision about a person we need to have a difficult conversation with. It may be a decision about inventory, a buying decision, or a strategic decision. These can be the quick, momentary prayers: "Lord, what do you think?"

Even after the pandemic ended, we found ourselves unable to get our inventory shipped to our warehouse. As a result, at one point we were down to only 60 percent of what we needed. Our trucks seemed to be stalled. We began to pray, and slowly, little by little, we saw the logjam begin to break. So every time I was out driving and saw a Hobby Lobby truck, I'd point at the truck and say, "Thank you, Lord." It was another way I could pray continually.

It is a good thing to be on our knees before God about our needs, but prayer is also about rejoicing in God's goodness and thanking Him for His sufficient grace. Prayer is a daily ongoing conversation we are having with God as we go along our way.

How can you practice continual prayer? What are things you can rejoice in every day? What are situations in your work and routine you can treat as an ongoing conversation with God? Write down several things you can be in prayer about daily.

The Downside of Too Many Choices

"Martha, Martha," the Lord answered, "you are worried and upset about many things, but few things are needed—or indeed only one. Mary has chosen what is better, and it will not be taken away from her."

Luke 10:41–42

Because we operate a thousand stores and stock thirty thousand seasonal items, there is always the risk of getting lost in a million decisions. To combat this pull toward making too many choices, we hung a sign in our Oklahoma City warehouse that says, "Keep it simple. CLOSE COUNTS! Too many choices are harmful to business."

It is the only sign in our entire complex with my name on it.

I feel strongly about moving away from the complexity of too many choices to the simplicity of fewer choices because I want to run one store a thousand times, not a thousand stores one at a time. But there is a more important reason, and it goes back to Jesus having dinner with a few good friends.

In Luke 10 we read about two sisters who both loved Jesus, Martha and Mary. On this occasion Jesus was in their home, probably enjoying a meal and meaningful conversation. But there was a problem. Martha was stressed. There was too much to do, too many decisions to make, and her sister wasn't offering to help. When Martha complained to Jesus, He replied, "Few things are needed—indeed only one."

While Martha was deciding what to do and how to do it, and worrying about missing something, Mary was making a decision too. But Mary was able to prioritize and limit her choices, and from those few things she believed were most important, she chose to sit at Jesus's feet and listen to Him.

Of all the things that worry and upset us at any given moment, how many of them are truly essential? In Matthew 6:33, Jesus promises that if we seek first His kingdom and His righteousness, everything we truly need will be supplied by our Father in heaven.

———

How could you limit the number of choices you make every day? How could you reduce the distractions? If you were to focus on five to ten truly essential decisions you need to make this week, what might they be?

Are You Building to Sell?

> Suppose one of you wants to build a tower. Won't you first sit down and estimate the cost to see if you have enough money to complete it?
>
> Luke 14:28

I have a friend who built a nice, solid company. There were lots of great employees, and they did lots of great things in the community. But eventually he sold it.

And that was his entire purpose. He'd built the company to sell it. He always knew that there was a sale on the horizon, which leads to the question, Why are you building?

Are you building to sell? There's nothing wrong with that. It just helps to know if that's your purpose. The things you're building aren't permanent. Someone will buy them, take over, and establish a new purpose.

Some build to split, which means building so everyone can have a share of the pie. Sometimes that means key leaders and officers. Often it means splitting up ownership among family members. They pass down ownership to their kids, who may give to their kids, and so on.

Without careful thought, the split could become permanent. There are just too many hands in the pie to make effective leadership decisions for the good of the organization.

Some build for purpose—for generations to come. It's hard work. To build for purpose means having a clear vision that gets people excited for the future. They've got to have a clear mission that tells people what they'll need to do every day to execute the vision. They've got to have clear values that provide guardrails for the work they undertake.

Not every organization can and should last for generations. But it comes back to the question, Why are you building? To sell? To split? For purpose?

———

How many building projects or real estate developments have you seen that never got completed? How did that reflect on the builders? What are the pros and cons of each method—build to sell, build to split, and build for purpose?

DAY 15

Dream Big, but Start Small

> Whoever can be trusted with very little can also be trusted with much, and whoever is dishonest with very little will also be dishonest with much.
>
> Luke 16:10

In 1970 Barbara and I borrowed $600 and began making miniature picture frames out of our home. She worked for free, and we paid our children seven cents to glue the frames together. It was a small beginning that, over time, led to a very big idea. Today Hobby Lobby employs over fifty thousand people in over one thousand stores and generates $8 billion in sales. How did that happen?

Let me be the first to assure you that it didn't happen because of how smart I am! No, every good thing that's happened in our family and business over the past fifty years came from the good hand of a gracious God.

And this same good and gracious God tells us in Luke 16 how He wants to partner with us to bring blessing. He entrusts us with small things, and if we steward them well, He then entrusts us with bigger things. Our job is to be faithful stewards of whatever God places in our hands; God's job is to enlarge our influence as we steward them well. Just think for a moment how Jesus took a boy's sack lunch (five small barley loaves and two fish) and multiplied it to feed over five thousand people. The boy was a faithful, generous steward of his food, and God made what he had grow exponentially to bless others.

But this truth cuts both ways: if we aren't faithful with little, we won't be entrusted with more. In fact, the little we have will be taken from us and given to others who have been faithful. If I would lie to my wife over a small thing to avoid embarrassment, I would also lie to her over big things—because lying reveals my character.

Do you have big dreams for God? I hope so! Keep dreaming big but remember to start small. God shapes your character and abilities first in small things, so do your very best with whatever He's placed in your hands today.

What "small things" has God given you responsibility for that could be easily overlooked? What are your big dreams? Be sure to write them down and share them with someone.

The Secret of Contentment

> I know what it is to be in need, and I know what it is to have plenty. I have learned the secret of being content in any and every situation, whether well fed or hungry, whether living in plenty or in want.
>
> Philippians 4:12

People sometimes think I'm crazy! When I tell business leaders that I make 5 percent of what other CEOs make, and we give 50 percent of our profits away, they wonder how that works. It doesn't compute in a world that tells us the path to happiness is more, more, and more.

The truth is, I have everything I need. This world doesn't offer anything more that I want. A bigger house? Another car? Another trip? Not for me. I am content. I've learned the secret Paul speaks of in Philippians 4, but it wasn't always this way. Nobody can simply tell you the secret of contentment; you have to learn it for yourself.

God has different ways to teach us this secret. Sometimes He gives us what we think we need to feel happy and satisfied, only for us to discover that it leaves us hungry for more. This happened to King Solomon, and you can read his cautionary tale in Ecclesiastes.

Sometimes God doesn't give us what we want, what we pray for, what we "must" have to be content. He prunes back good things from our lives until we're left with just Him, and that's when we discover He's enough. This is how Paul learned the secret. We see part of his learning process in 2 Corinthians 12, when he prayed three times for God to remove a thorn in his flesh but God said no. After a struggle, Paul found contentment in God's sufficient grace, even though he didn't get what he asked for.

I find that what makes me most content is when I consider all the people who don't know Jesus—people who will be eternally separated from God. When I consider the vast spiritual need in the world, it keeps me focused on what others truly need and content with what I have.

———

Are you a content person? Have you learned the secret yet? When do you feel the most discontent? What do those feelings reveal about where you're looking for contentment?

Building for 150 Years

> Know therefore that the Lord your God is God; he is the faithful God, keeping his covenant of love to a thousand generations of those who love him and keep his commandments.
>
> Deuteronomy 7:9

Do you remember the hit movie *National Treasure*? Nicholas Cage, as Ben Gates, with his unlikely accomplice, Riley Poole, steal the Declaration of Independence. But in contemplating his coming theft, Gates quotes the words of the document: "It is their right, it is their duty, to throw off such Government, and provide new Guards for their future security."*

Gates then says simply, "People don't talk like that anymore."

And it's true. People don't talk like that anymore. We tend to not think of the larger good, the welfare of the community over the individual, the narrative of the generations.

Our view tends to be short-term. We focus on what's good for us right now, in this moment.

---

* *National Treasure*, directed by Jon Turteltaub (Burbank, CA: Walt Disney Home Entertainment, 2004), DVD.

I think that's particularly true in America, where our history is relatively short—not even three hundred years old. Go to Europe or Asia, for instance, and you'll see houses, banks, and streets that are literally hundreds of years old. These communities understand history. They understand the concept of generations.

Contemplate that for a minute. Think about the generations that have gone before you—your parents, grandparents, great-grandparents. How far back can you go? Then think about future generations. Your children. Your grandchildren. Your great-grandchildren?

Think five to ten generations ahead. What would it look like if these descendants were all a people of faith, a people who loved big ideas and lived lives of honor?

Generational families change the world.

———

How far back can you go in thinking through your own family tree? What were the noble accomplishments or perhaps the challenges the family faced? As you contemplate future generations in your family tree, what are the ideas and values you'd most want them to reflect in 150 years?

Only God Can Promote You

> No one from the east or the west or from the desert can exalt themselves. It is God who judges: He brings one down, he exalts another.
>
> Psalm 75:6–7

Early in my career, I worked for TG&Y, a variety store chain. During my thirteen years there, I saw some people promoted, others passed over, and some fired. I was promoted to store manager and enjoyed the additional opportunities and responsibilities. I did my best, albeit not perfectly, to work hard and treat people with respect.

But God didn't leave me there. He chose to promote me to cofound Hobby Lobby alongside Barbara. And that raises a question: Why does God promote some people to positions of greater influence? Why did God promote me? Was it because I was smarter or somehow better than anyone else? Not likely.

Joseph's life gives us an important clue about why God promotes people to positions of influence, and it's this principle: "Whatever you do, work at it with all your heart, as working for the Lord" (Col. 3:23).

40

While a slave in Egypt, Joseph refused to sleep with Potiphar's wife (Gen. 39). His refusal enraged her, and she accused him of attempted rape, which led to his demotion to prison.

While in prison, Joseph proved himself so faithful and capable that he was put in charge of the other prisoners. When asked to interpret the dreams of two fellow prisoners, he told them both the truth, even though it meant bad news for one of them. His honesty and hard work led to a promotion to Pharaoh's chief of staff (Gen. 40–41).

God demoted Joseph in the first instance and promoted him in the second—even though Joseph was faithful in both circumstances. God positioned Joseph perfectly in prison to set the stage for the big promotion that was coming. Joseph had no way of knowing this at the time. God raises up and God brings down, for His own reasons and in His own timing, but always for our good.

Have you ever experienced a demotion of some kind that was God's setup for a bigger promotion He wanted for you? If so, what did you learn from this? Opportunity came to Joseph while he was being faithful in a difficult circumstance. What does faithfulness look like for you this week?

Stepping into the Waters of Faith

> And as soon as the priests who carry the ark of the Lord—
> the Lord of all the earth—set foot in the Jordan, its waters
> flowing downstream will be cut off and stand up in a heap.
>
> Joshua 3:13

One of the first times I heard God speaking directly to me took place on my return flight from our denomination's convention. The Holy Spirit clearly said, *You need to give $30,000 for Bible literature.* The year was 1979, and Hobby Lobby was barely turning a profit.

Barbara and I wanted to give generously to literature ministries, but we simply didn't have $30,000. Why would God ask us to do the impossible?

Well, as it turns out, God makes a habit of asking people to do the impossible—with incredible results! In Joshua 3, God asks Israel to cross the Jordan River to take possession of the land He promised to Abraham. How could millions of people with all their possessions and livestock cross a river without a bridge or boats? Impossible!

But the God of the Bible is never fazed by impossibilities. He tells the priests to go first and carry the ark into the Jordan. They listen to God's Word and simply obey, not knowing what to expect. As soon as they step into the river, carrying the ark on their shoulders, the water stops flowing. Soon they're standing on rocks and silty sand and the entire nation passes through to the other side.

God asks for a step of obedience first, and then He shows up and does what only He can do.

Barbara and I took our step of faith by writing a check for $7,500 and trusting God for the rest—and He showed up! We ended up giving $30,000, and God expanded our imaginations for what He wanted to do through our giving.

What impossible thing is God asking you to do? What could be your first step of obedience as you respond in faith to how God is speaking to you?

The Black Sheep of the Family

> Then the Lord said to Moses, "See, I have chosen Bezalel son of Uri, the son of Hur, of the tribe of Judah, and I have filled him with the Spirit of God, with wisdom, with understanding, with knowledge and with all kinds of skills—to make artistic designs for work in gold, silver and bronze."
>
> Exodus 31:1–4

All five of my siblings either became pastors or married pastors. My father was a pastor, and our mother served faithfully at his side for decades. I was the only one who didn't go into vocational ministry, and for a long time I thought I was the black sheep of the family.

Maybe you work in business, teach in a school, or fight fires, and you wonder if what you do really matters as much as preaching sermons or leading ministries. Does God really call people to weld axles and write code?

Consider Bezalel. In Exodus 31, God gives instructions through Moses for the building of the tabernacle—the place where God would meet and be with His people. And one man is singled out, called out by God for a special assignment. His name is Bezalel. He's filled with the Spirit of God—not to preach or teach. He's anointed with the gift of metalworking. God uses him and his special skill set to help build the tabernacle.

I suspect that Bezalel never thought of himself as particularly special. He wasn't a leader like Moses or Aaron. He was just doing what God put in front of him, working metal. Over time, he became good at it, and as he worked at it, he enjoyed it. That's the way it works. God puts something in front of you. It may not seem special or different. But as you work at it, you become good at it, and you begin to sense God's design for you.

God called me into business and anointed me to be a merchant. But it started when I was a stock boy in a little five-and-dime in Altus, Oklahoma. As I am faithful to my calling, I can rest assured God will be honored through my work and my life, and people will be blessed by God through me. And you can rest assured too.

———

What is your calling? How has the Holy Spirit anointed you to fulfill your calling? How can you share the good news about Jesus through your nine-to-five job?

45

Getting Your Hands Dirty

After saying this, he spit on the ground, made some mud
with the saliva, and put it on the man's eyes. "Go," he told
him, "wash in the Pool of Siloam" (this word means "Sent").
So the man went and washed, and came home seeing.

John 9:6–7

T. Texas Tyler was my first business mentor. One day he asked
me to clean the toilets, and I was less than excited. Realizing my
lack of both experience and enthusiasm for the task at hand,
he rolled up his sleeves and showed me how to properly clean
a toilet. He literally got his hands dirty to help me succeed.

Jesus wasn't afraid to get His hands dirty either. In John 9,
He healed a man born blind, but instead of simply saying, "Be
healed!" He spit in the dirt, made some mud, and rubbed it on
the man's eyes. Jesus regularly modeled this "down in the dirt"
approach with His followers. He wasn't a scholar hanging out
in a fancy office; He was down in the streets touching lepers,
healing those with diseases and sickness.

I admire that. It would be easy for me to stay in my plush
CEO's office. But I find that I enjoy my day the most when I'm

out in the warehouse or inside our stores, working with our people. The bigger the organization, the easier it is to get distanced from working on the front lines. How long has it been since you got your hands dirty?

Here are a few suggestions to spark your imagination:

1. Arrive to a meeting early or stay late to help set up or tear down the room.
2. Slow down and listen to the questions or concerns of a team member.
3. Take extra time to make sure you give good instructions on work to be done.

For me, I've found that as long as I remember to be in the weeds, my passion for the people and the ministry of the organization remains high. And I like to remember that Jesus not only got His hands dirty, He got them bloody. He was the ultimate model of self-sacrifice.

———

What opportunities do you have to get your hands dirty at work? What may God be asking you to sacrifice to love and serve your people well?

The Blessing and Curse of Wealth

A good person leaves an inheritance for their children's children, but a sinner's wealth is stored up for the righteous.

Proverbs 13:22

Has God given you the ability to generate wealth? Wealth can be a tool to bless future generations, but it can also be a curse that harms your children and grandchildren.

As of the writing of this book, I'm eighty-one years old, so I've spent a lot of time thinking about this question. What will Barbara and I do with the wealth God has given us? How can we use it as a tool for blessing and protect our family from its corrosive effects?

Proverbs 13 says good people leave an inheritance for their grandchildren. What kind of inheritance do you want to leave? Our prayer is to first pass down these things:

- Love for God.
- Love for God's Word.

- Loving people through sharing the gospel.
- Working hard at whatever God gives you to do.

Everyone can pass down these forms of wealth. Wealth is far more than money. But when it comes to financial wealth, our goal is to make financial gifts to our children while we are still alive. We like the idea of making these gifts now to benefit them when they still have a need for it. For us, these are relatively smaller amounts that are designed to encourage them but still provide an incentive to work.

At Hobby Lobby, we provide an opportunity for our children to work and enter the business. But no one, including me, can get paid by Hobby Lobby unless they work for the company. No one will inherit an interest in the company.

We realize that our approach to inheritance is not for everyone. In our case we are guided by Proverbs 20:21, which says, "An inheritance claimed too soon will not be blessed at the end." We've seen families torn apart by money passed down without proper training. Wealth without wisdom can be a curse.

We don't want inheritance to be a windfall but instead an opportunity to create more growth and opportunity for God's kingdom. How can you leverage your wealth to bless not only your family but others who need to see and hear about the love of Christ?

How can the wealth God has given you today bless your great-great-grandchildren? What safeguards can you erect now to prevent your wealth from harming your family?

Making the Ask

> You desire but do not have, so you kill. You covet but you cannot get what you want, so you quarrel and fight. You do not have because you do not ask God. When you ask, you do not receive, because you ask with wrong motives, that you may spend what you get on your pleasures.
>
> James 4:2–3

During a financial crisis at Hobby Lobby, we called our family together. It was a very difficult time. I had to admit to our children and grandchildren that we were in trouble and I didn't know how we could get through it. I was humbled like I'd never been humbled before. And that's when our oldest son, Mart, said, "Dad, we aren't depending on you. We're depending on the Lord."

As a family, we agreed to move forward in dependence on the Lord, not on ourselves. We asked God to do what seemed like the impossible: to right the ship and move us back into the black. And God answered those prayers. We were profitable again the following year.

Where are you depending on yourself, your own wisdom, or your own resources to get you through instead of asking God for help? I understand how difficult it is to confess your mistakes, your pride, and your feelings of helplessness. It's embarrassing and agonizing to die to our arrogance and self-reliance.

Yet God has so many good things He wants to give us, ways He wants to grow us, and people He wants to bless through us. But He won't force Himself upon anyone; we must ask Him for the things we need and, yes, even the things we want.

If we fail to ask God for those things with humility and gratitude, we will move toward violence, conflict, and jealousy (James 4). If we don't ask God for what we want, we won't get it, period.

What are you trying to handle on your own that you need to start asking for God's help with? Who do you need to bring together to confess your dependency upon God and invite to join you in prayer?

For Such a Time as This

For if you remain silent at this time, relief and deliverance for the Jews will arise from another place, but you and your father's family will perish. And who knows but that you have come to your royal position for such a time as this?

Esther 4:14

In 2014 we found ourselves embroiled in a legal pressure cooker that went all the way to the US Supreme Court. According to new government regulations, we were required to provide certain contraceptives as part of our health insurance that violated our conscience, because we believed they stopped the creation of life after an egg was fertilized. This we could not do.

Many in the press demonized us and called us "women-haters." The attacks were painful, unrelenting, and continue to this day. But even more sobering was the very real possibility that Hobby Lobby would face financial ruin if the Supreme Court ruled in favor of the government. What would happen to our thousands of employees and their families?

The risks were huge, but we couldn't remain silent. Like Esther, who risked her life by speaking up to protect her fellow

Jews, we realized that God had placed us in this position for such a time as this.

God answered our prayers, and the Supreme Court ruled in our favor. It wasn't only a victory for Hobby Lobby but for countless Christian business leaders who share our convictions.

You have influence. God has placed you in a position that impacts the lives of people—whether you're a CEO or administrative assistant or bricklayer. Are you remaining silent about something that, deep in your heart, you know God wants you to speak up about? Maybe it involves how people are being treated, a lapse in integrity, or mission drift.

You have been placed exactly where you are by God for such a time as this. What do you want to do with that opportunity?

Is God stirring your heart about anything as you read this today? Can you name what it is? What might God want you to say? Who could you discuss this with to help discern what you could say and how best to say it?

Beware of Success

> The Israelites sampled their provisions but did not inquire of the Lord.
>
> Joshua 9:14

One of your greatest enemies can be your success.

Israel was on a winning streak. They'd already conquered Jericho with nothing more than a seven-day march around the city and a trumpet blast. And while the Israelites had a temporary slip in their streak, they'd also finished off the city of Ai pretty quickly.

The news of their success spread. The Bible carefully records that the message spread from the hill country to the foothills, and all the way to the seacoast. Pretty much everywhere. The surrounding nations were afraid that Israel would soon overtake them.

The Gibeonites were one of those nations. They saw the advance of the Israelites and, fearing they'd soon lose their own battle, chose a plan of action. They concocted a scheme to pretend they were from a far country. They showed up at Israel's front door with worn-out shoes, worn-out clothes, worn-out wineskins, and moldy bread. They said they'd heard of Israel's power and wanted them to sign a treaty to not conquer them.

It was all a scam. But Israel's success kept them from seeing the truth. They didn't stop and pray. They just acted on their own without consulting the God who had brought them their first two wins. It was almost as if they expected to keep winning because *they* were good. So they signed the treaty.

And that's what I've always found. My success can get in the way of my prayer and my dependence on God. When I stop praying, I start thinking the wins are mine and that the wins will certainly continue. That's when the real danger starts.

———

Have you ever had a time where you made a rash decision and realized that further reflection would have avoided the mistake? What do you think was going through the mind of Joshua when he accepted the treaty and chose not to question the Gibeonites' story further?

Can You Miss Your Calling?

When the LORD saw that he had gone over to look, God called to him from within the bush, "Moses! Moses!" And Moses said, "Here I am."

Exodus 3:4

As I mentioned earlier, I was the only one of my siblings who did not go into full-time ministry. Did I miss my calling? Did I make a mistake by going into business instead of going to seminary?

I've asked myself that question a few times over the years, but God always affirms that my calling is to be a merchant. Not just any merchant, but one who loves God with everything I have and loves the people He entrusts to my care.

You may sometimes wonder if you've missed God's calling. If so, you're in good company; so did Moses. As a young man raised with all the advantages that come with being a member of a royal family, Moses was in a powerful position to do something big for God.

When he first embraced his calling at age forty, it was a disaster. He killed an Egyptian who was abusing a Hebrew slave, and when his crime was discovered, he had to run for his life. Moses had yet to learn that God's calling on our lives can only be realized through God's power and in God's timing.

For another forty years, he wandered the desert as a shepherd. How many lonely nights did he spend regretting his rashness and anger? How often did he berate himself for missing his chance? But then, when Moses was eighty, God called to him from a burning bush and reinstated and expanded his calling.

Be encouraged today by these elements of Moses's story:

- You are never too old to be called by God.
- When God is ready to get your attention and speak to you, He knows exactly how to do it.
- No matter what mistakes you've made in the past, you are never beyond God's desire and ability to use you.

When you were a young Christian, did you have a sense of something important God was calling you to do? What was it? Like Moses, are you being called by God back to that vision somehow? What obstacles or failures might be holding you back from pursuing what God has called you to?

Shepherd Your Flock

Be shepherds of God's flock that is under your care, watching over them—not because you must, but because you are willing, as God wants you to be; not pursuing dishonest gain, but eager to serve; not lording it over those entrusted to you, but being examples to the flock.

1 Peter 5:2–3

As God blessed Hobby Lobby and we opened more stores, we had to hire more people. We now have over fifty thousand employees. Each of these individuals is created in God's image, is loved by God, and has a soul that will live forever. Even though I am not their pastor, I feel a responsibility to do all within my power to help them and their families experience the abundant life Jesus came to give each of us.

So, in that sense, I see them as part of my flock. As I've tried to lead our team in following the example of the Good Shepherd, we've made a few major decisions:

- We will be closed on Sundays so our people can rest and go to church with their families.

- We will close by 8:00 p.m. every day and limit our store hours to sixty-six per week.
- We will pay our employees more than the industry average.
- We will share our faith in Christ honestly.

In 1 Peter 5 we are reminded that good undershepherds (pastors and elders) are characterized by their willingness to watch over their people, to serve rather than enrich themselves from their flock, to treat people with respect, and to be a good example. If God has called you to serve Him in business, has He called you to do the same?

I wonder how much difference it makes to see ourselves as shepherds of our employees and teams. Shepherds have the responsibility to preserve and protect. They make sure their sheep get fed, and they help their sheep along the path.

As you think about your role in leading other people, what's your perspective? Is it the perspective of a shepherd?

Have you ever worked for someone who took excellent care of their employees and influenced them toward Christ? What did they do that you might imitate? What is one practical way you can better shepherd your flock this week?

Your Vapor Life

> You do not know what your life will be like tomorrow. For you are just a vapor that appears for a little while, and then vanishes away.
>
> James 4:14 NASB

Barbara and I began building picture frames in our garage over fifty years ago, but it feels like yesterday. I can still close my eyes and smell the sawdust and see our children gluing those frames. So much has happened since then. God has been so good to our family and our business. But it all happened in a blink. Looking back, I am reminded that our lives are like a vapor. We are here for a short time, and then we vanish.

Have you made peace with the reality of your vapor life? If you're in your twenties or thirties, you may not have thought much about this yet. It may feel like you'll have lots of time to worry about such things later. But the sooner we come to grips with these fundamental truths, the sooner we can prioritize what's most important and start investing in what will truly last.

These biblical truths are:

- None of us have the promise of tomorrow. This life could end at any moment.
- Our lives are like a vapor or mist that is here today but will quickly vanish.
- God created us with eternity in our hearts; we have souls that will live forever.
- God's Word is eternal; it will never fade away.
- Jesus offers us eternal life. When we trust Him and receive Him by faith, we share in His never-ending life.

Pause for a moment and allow these truths to sink in. If we really believe and take to heart these five declarations, they will impact every aspect of our lives—personally and professionally.

When you reflect upon your vapor life, does anything come to mind that you want to do more of? Are there things you want to do less of? What are they? How can you start investing more time and resources into those things that will last beyond this lifetime? What is one change you want to make over the next six months?

Did God Lose His GPS?

So God led the people around by the desert road toward the Red Sea. The Israelites went up out of Egypt ready for battle.

Exodus 13:18

Sometimes following God just feels wrong. Have you ever had a feeling you were driving the wrong way, even though you were following the directions? In 2018, we felt led by the Lord to discontinue selling Halloween items. Personally, I had fond memories of trick-or-treating as a boy, and something about pulling those items didn't feel good. Even though we were clear on where God was leading us, it was a tough decision.

I wondered, *Why would God lead us to walk away from millions of dollars in sales that could help fund His work around the world?*

Not everywhere God leads us makes sense at the time. Sometimes we may even wonder if God is lost or confused. Rest assured, God isn't directionally challenged.

But that's exactly what many Israelites probably thought when God led them out of their bondage in Egypt and straight to the Red Sea. They found themselves trapped, with Pharaoh's army in hot pursuit.

As panic began to set in, Moses shouted, "Do not be afraid. Stand firm and you will see the deliverance the LORD will bring you today" (Exod. 14:13).

As it turns out, God had two very good reasons to lead Israel to the Red Sea. First, He knew they weren't ready for the battles that would have ensued had they taken any other route. And second, He wanted everyone to see His power in delivering His people and defeating their enemies, so Israel would fear the Lord and learn to trust Him and Moses.

God also has very good reasons why He led us to pull out of Halloween merchandise, even though the decision didn't make financial sense. When we follow His lead, we are choosing not to allow fear to determine our course but to stand firm in God's salvation for our family and our employees.

Has God ever led you to do something that simply didn't make sense on paper but turned out to be a blessing in the end? If so, what did you learn through that experience? Are you facing a tough decision right now that makes you feel anxious? How can you stand firm in your faith?

Get into the Weeds

> Be sure you know the condition of your flocks, give careful attention to your herds; for riches do not endure forever, and a crown is not secure for all generations.
>
> Proverbs 27:23–24

I spent a season as CEO doing what most CEOs do. I worked to put a great team in place, helped them in their roles, and kept an eye on the trends that impacted our industry. Some people call that "working on the business." But I found myself too far removed, flying at thirty thousand feet. Honestly, I was bored. I needed to get back into the weeds.

I went back to doing what I do best: merchandising. I love merchandising so much I still work full-time and come in on most Saturdays for a half day. Part of what I enjoy about finding the best possible merchandise at the best prices for our customers is getting my hands dirty. I am one of those leaders who wants to get directly involved in the nitty-gritty of the organization. I got out of the weeds for a season to get a bird's-eye view, but it wasn't for me.

Proverbs 27 exhorts every leader to pay close attention to the condition of their herds (or their business). The warning

64

is that if you get too caught up in the big picture, or forecasting which way the economy is heading, or studying the best practices of other business leaders, you can easily lose focus on what's most important. When that happens, companies learn the hard way that "riches do not endure forever."

Some leaders feel their time is too important to attend certain meetings, ask new hires how they are doing, or be involved in the day-to-day operations. They prefer to delegate those responsibilities to others while they operate at higher altitudes. But good leaders must roll up their sleeves and get into the weeds from time to time to know firsthand how the herd is really doing.

What would "getting into the weeds" look like for you? Do you need to be more intentional about seeing the entire forest, or getting close to the trees? Which of your responsibilities do you need to carry personally, even though they could be delegated?

How God Turns Us Around

"The time has come," he said. "The kingdom of God has come near. Repent and believe the good news!"

Mark 1:15

On a few occasions God grabbed my attention to dramatically change the way we do things at Hobby Lobby. In the mid-1980s God turned me around personally regarding my pride and organizationally regarding our long-term debt. My tearful admission to our family that I didn't know what to do when the banks threatened foreclosure and our decision to eliminate long-term debt were both game changers. We wouldn't be who we are today if God hadn't turned us around and put us on a different path.

But how does it work? How do we know when God is speaking to us and asking us to reverse course? Jesus's first words in the book of Mark provide important clues.

First, Jesus says the time has come. The Greek word translated "time" here, *kairos*, isn't chronological time but instead carries the idea of the "right time" or the "fullness of time." God decides when the time is right to speak and to invite us into a needed course correction.

Second, He says the kingdom of God has come near. Remember what the disciples just witnessed at Jesus's baptism? The heavens opened, God the Father spoke, and the Holy Spirit descended as a dove upon Jesus. God's kingdom, which had been there all along, literally broke through into their conscious awareness.

In His perfect timing, God gets our attention by breaking through into our awareness with a message. It may be an event, a pattern that becomes painfully obvious, an opportunity, or even an illness or setback. It usually includes the sensation of someone shaking us awake.

And while the details constantly change, the message always carries these two elements: repentance and belief. To repent means to change your mind, your direction, or your course. To believe means to trust God enough to take action. In other words, you hear what God says and then actively respond in faith and obedience.

Has God been getting your attention as of late? Is now the right time to pay special attention to what God may be saying to you? What areas of your life or business need to turn around?

The Secret about Wealth

> You may say to yourself, "My power and the strength of my hands have produced this wealth for me." But remember the LORD your God, for it is he who gives you the ability to produce wealth.
>
> Deuteronomy 8:17–18

As of today's writing, the richest person in the world is a French business owner named Bernard Arnault. His net worth is estimated at $202 billion. That's a staggering amount of wealth. No doubt he's a smart man who has worked very hard, but did he amass all that wealth by himself? Can he truly say, "Look what I've accomplished!"?

As Israel prepared to enter the land God promised to Abraham, Moses reminded them of this fundamental truth in Deuteronomy 8: *only God gives the ability to produce wealth*.

Some of us have been blessed by God to produce wealth. But rather than strutting around like peacocks expecting people to admire our intelligence and entrepreneurial acumen, we should be the most humble, grateful, and generous people on the planet.

Think about it for just a moment.

- Who determined when you would be born? (You could have launched your business on October 28, 1929. That was the day the stock market crashed and ignited the Great Depression.)
- Who determined where you would be born? (You could have been born in a country where the average person makes around $300 per year.)
- Who determined which family you were born into? (You could have been born into wealth or poverty.)
- Who determines whether you will wake up tomorrow morning and get out of bed? (Jesus says that none of us have the promise of tomorrow.)

Since only God can give us the ability and opportunity to produce wealth, and since it all belonged to Him before we showed up and will still be His after we're gone, shouldn't we view wealth as something we steward and a tool to bless people and point them to Christ?

———

If you've been blessed to produce wealth (by which I mean more resources than are required to meet your fundamental needs), how do you view it? What can you do with that wealth to bless others and honor God?

We Sow It, God Grows It

> I planted the seed, Apollos watered it, but God has been making it grow. So neither the one who plants nor the one who waters is anything, but only God, who makes things grow.
>
> 1 Corinthians 3:6–7

We want to sow God's Word into our employees' hearts and water those seeds with grace and truth. Like Paul and Apollos, our responsibility as leaders is to sow and water God's Word as we trust God to make it grow.

What are a few practical ways we've done this over the years?

- At our corporate headquarters, we have a small staff of chaplains our employees can visit while on the clock.
- We offer a variety of marriage and family classes.
- We encourage management staff to take advantage of an all-expenses-paid marriage conference.

These efforts are designed to serve our people at their point of need, whether it's in marriage, finances, or just counsel for their life. We hope that as we serve they'll be pointed to the hope of Jesus.

Even with all the resources out in the community, I think we underestimate people's vast needs in the basics of daily life: having good relationships, raising children, having a healthy marriage, dealing with debt, and managing a budget. These are all big issues. Can you imagine what it must feel like to face them without God, the Bible, or a healthy spiritual community? Our challenge is to learn how to best respond to the needs of those entrusted to our care.

Every situation is different, and bringing in chaplains may not work for you. A good resource is a book by J. Frank Harrison called *The Transformation Factor: Leading Your Company for Good, for God, and for Growth.* We sow and water God's Word by speaking it with our lips and our lives, and then we ask God to do what only He can do: make the seed come to life and bring transformation.

———

What opportunities do you have to sow and water God's Word at work? How can you more intentionally and naturally integrate God's Word into your company culture?

The Problem with Comparisons

Each one should test their own actions. Then they can take pride in themselves alone, without comparing themselves to someone else, for each one should carry their own load.

Galatians 6:4–5

As I've mentioned, Hobby Lobby is an $8 billion company with over a thousand stores and fifty thousand employees. When I drop by a small mom-and-pop corner store with one location, two employees, and peeling paint, I can feel pretty good about myself and what we've accomplished. It would be easy to be prideful.

But then if I read an article telling me that Apple made $122 billion in 2022, I can feel deflated. In fact, I can feel jealous and downright depressed.

You see the problem with comparisons. On the one hand, we can become puffed up with pride, and on the other hand, we can become discouraged and ungrateful. Paul instructs Christians in Galatians 6 to not compare themselves to anyone else.

Instead he encourages them to take pride in their own work and carry their own load.

God has given us an assignment, a calling that is tailor-made just for us. He also gives each of us gifts and opportunities to fulfill that calling—to joyfully carry the load we were intended to bear. He wants us to experience the satisfaction of knowing that whatever we do, however big or small in comparison to someone else, makes a difference. It's important. We are colaborers with Christ.

Sometimes I'm asked to give speeches at events. But it's not something I love to do. I'm amazed at men and women who can hold thousands of people spellbound, straining to hear their every word. But I am not one of those people. God has called and gifted me to be a merchandiser.

Whether we own one store or ten thousand, it doesn't really matter. The important question to ask ourselves is, *Am I doing whatever God has given me to do with my whole heart?*

Are you faithfully stewarding whatever He has entrusted to you?

———

Have you ever felt overly inflated or deflated when you compared yourself with someone else? How did that experience go for you? Do you have clarity on what your load is? What can you do this week to focus on what God has given you and steward it well?

Bold Prayer and Divine Intervention

> I will place a wool fleece on the threshing floor. If there is dew only on the fleece and all the ground is dry, then I will know that you will save Israel by my hand, as you said.
>
> Judges 6:37

There have been many important decisions I've made over the years relating to our family or our business that I lacked the information or wisdom to make with confidence. Even after praying for God's direction, I still felt unsure about which way to go. Can you relate?

Whether it was a decision about a business we wanted to purchase, suing the federal government, or making a gift of some size, the best choice hasn't always been obvious.

Gideon faced a terrible choice in Judges 6 that was literally life or death. Should he lead a small band of soldiers to attack a vastly superior Midianite army, or would it be better to play it safe and live to fight another day? In the end, he asked God for a sign. He put a sheep's fleece on the ground and asked that the ground be dry and the fleece be covered with dew by morning. God did as he asked. Still uncertain of what to do, Gideon repeated his request, but this time asked for wet ground and a dry fleece. Again, God answered.

Are you wrestling with a decision right now? Do you need more assurance from God one way or the other before you can make the best possible choice? What is it you need from God? Gideon was bold in his request. Perhaps you can make a similar bold request in faith.

God knew Gideon's heart. He knew Gideon wanted to understand and obey His will. But He also knew Gideon's frailty and insecurity. To attack the army of Midian without God's direct intervention would be suicide. So God gave him what he needed, and He will do the same for you.

———

What is a big decision you are wrestling with today? In your heart, do you really want to know God's will and do it with God's help, no matter what? If so, what bold prayer do you need to bring before the Lord?

Test Yourself: Are You a Steward or an Owner?

> Naked I came from my mother's womb, and naked I will de-part. The LORD gave and the LORD has taken away; may the name of the LORD be praised.
>
> Job 1:21

I've talked with thousands of Christian business owners and ministry leaders about biblical stewardship. When it comes to acknowledging God's ownership over everything they have, even the breath that fills their lungs at that moment, they all agree: "Yes, God owns it all. We are called to be faithful stewards."

It's one thing to say you are a steward and God is the owner, but it's another thing to live it out. Here's a good question to ask yourself: *What if it all burned to the ground tonight?*

What would happen to you, to your sense of identity and security as God's beloved son or daughter, if your business or ministry literally burned to the ground and no longer existed when you woke up tomorrow morning?

After absorbing the initial shock, how would you respond?

- Would you still trust God's love and goodness in spite of the serious setback?
- Would you feel crushed, cheated, and in despair?
- Would you grieve the loss but come back to God with an attitude that says, "Okay, what do you want to do from here?"

Most of us would feel a mixture of those responses and more; I know I certainly would. We read in Job 1 how a godly man responded to the loss of his fortune and his children. He of course was devastated by the news but somehow managed to keep his balance by acknowledging three core truths of stewardship:

1. We begin life naked and we end life naked; we take nothing of this world with us to the next.
2. God gives and God takes away, but His abiding presence and grace are always sufficient.
3. God is worthy to be praised in every circumstance, even intense suffering.

How could acknowledging God's ownership of your work and ministry give you more freedom and peace? What is one thing you can do this week to move toward a stewardship identity?

DAY 37

"Yes," "No," and "Wait"

> I remain confident of this: I will see the goodness of the LORD in the land of the living. Wait for the LORD; be strong and take heart and wait for the LORD.
>
> Psalm 27:13–14

I grew up in a family that prayed. My mother in particular was a woman of prayer. My wife, Barbara, regularly gets up in the middle of the night to pray for people all over the world, and she records those prayers and God's answers in a journal. I make it my ambition to pray about everything all day long. The Bible encourages us to pray without ceasing.

Naturally, when we pray about something big or small, we want God to say yes. And, in God's infinite grace and mercy, He often does just that. But not all the time. God isn't a genie in a bottle waiting to grant us our every wish and whim. He loves us far too much for that.

Sometimes God says no. Every good parent has to say no to their children. When your two-year-old daughter wants to play in the street, you say no. When your sixteen-year-old son wants to buy a muscle car, you say no. (At least the rest of us hope you do!) And when we ask God for certain things that seem important to us, He sometimes says no. He is a good and wise parent, and not everything we want is beneficial for us in the long run.

But sometimes God says neither yes or no. These are difficult times for us because our requests are met with silence. And in that silence, the best reply we can discern is simply *wait*.

In Psalm 27, David speaks of his desire to see God's goodness this side of heaven. He was bold enough to ask God to do some awesome things. But David understood the importance of waiting on God, knowing that many of his prayers would be answered according to God's timeline, not his own.

Waiting isn't for the weak. It takes strength and courage to wait for God, neither giving up nor forcing something to happen.

———

What prayers are you waiting on God to answer? How can you keep your strength and courage up in the waiting? What do you find most challenging in submitting to God's timing?

What Will Matter One Hundred Years from Now?

> Do not store up for yourselves treasures on earth, where moths and vermin destroy, and where thieves break in and steal. But store up for yourselves treasures in heaven. . . . For where your treasure is, there your heart will be also.
>
> Matthew 6:19–21

Did you know that the average lifespan of an S&P 500 company is only fifteen years, as of the writing of this book? That's an 80 percent decrease over the past eighty years.* The old saying must be true: "They just don't build them like they used to."

In an economy that is fueled by "planned obsolescence," where things are intentionally not built to last (just think about your car or your washer and dryer), it's hard to think one hundred years into the future. But just for a moment, let's give it a try.

What will matter to you one hundred years from now? If God continues to grant me good health, I will see my one

---

* Alex Hill, Liz Mellon, and Jules Goddard, "How Winning Organizations Last 100 Years," *Harvard Business Review*, September 27, 2018, https://hbr.org/2018/09/how-winning-organizations-last-100-years.

hundredth birthday in less than nineteen years. But a hundred years after that I will be long gone. Here is what I imagine will matter most to me:

- I will be in the presence of Jesus and many family members and friends who have joined me on the other side.
- I will have meaningful work to do in the new heaven and new earth (sitting on a cloud playing the harp all day doesn't sound like heaven to me!).
- I will worship God with all my strength.
- I will hear reports from time to time, as others join me, about how my great-great-great-grandchildren are serving God and living for Him.
- I will meet a few people who came to faith in Christ in some small part because of my witness.
- I will continue to read, study, and meditate on God's Word, and understand it in a far richer and deeper way.

What will matter most to you? Jesus promises if we value the eternal, we will have treasure in heaven that no stock market crash can ever take away.

———

What do you see when you imagine your life one hundred years from now? How might that vision help you to prioritize your life today? What does how you invest your time and money reveal about what your heart treasures?

Ashamed of the Gospel?

> For I am not ashamed of the gospel, because it is the power of God that brings salvation to everyone who believes: first to the Jew, then to the Gentile.
>
> Romans 1:16

What do you do with the opportunities God gives you to tell people about Jesus in your business? In our current cultural environment, there's a great deal of pressure to remain silent about our faith in Christ and effectively leave the gospel at home and in church.

But Jesus can't be put in a box. He goes with us wherever we go and is always at work calling people into a relationship with God that offers a transformed life today and a blessed eternity. The first time we included an opportunity for employees to respond to a gospel invitation at a comanager meeting, our general counsel was concerned we could be sued. He warned me this could cost us a lot of money.

I replied, "Fifteen people gave their lives to Christ today. You tell me—what is the cost of a soul?"

We continue to take the risk of giving employees an opportunity to place their faith in Christ in our comanager meetings, people continue to respond to the gospel, and thus far we haven't received a single complaint. But the risk is real, and the day may come when we do pay a price for sharing the gospel.

Paul tells us that the gospel is the power of God that brings salvation to everyone who believes. It was this same gospel that brought God's power into your life and into my life. Where would you be today without God's salvation that came to you through the gospel?

Rather than living in fear of what others may say or think, isn't it time for all of us to join Paul in unashamedly identifying with the gospel of Christ?

Have you ever felt ashamed of the gospel? If so, what did you learn from that experience? Have you had a personal experience of the life-transforming work of the gospel, the power of God, to save you? If not, who can you talk to about this?

No Regrets

> For I am already being poured out like a drink offering, and the time for my departure is near. I have fought the good fight, I have finished the race, I have kept the faith.
>
> 2 Timothy 4:6–7

When I was a young man in my twenties, my boss said to me, "The most important thing is your job, because your family's going to leave you one day." Looking back on it, that was probably the worst advice anyone has ever given me! I would never tell someone at Hobby Lobby that the most important thing in their life is their job.

When *Inc.* magazine interviewed entrepreneurs, asking about their biggest regrets, the number one response was "not spending enough time with friends and family."* Can you imagine anyone on their deathbed regretting not spending more time at the office or jobsite? Of course not! When the end of our life draws near, we realize what's most important.

---

* Lolly Daskal, "12 Things People Regret the Most Before They Die," *Inc.*, August 3, 2015, https://www.inc.com/lolly-daskal/12-things-people-regret -the-most-before-they-die.html.

In Paul's final words to his spiritual son Timothy, he reminds us of what is truly important. Paul probably had very few regrets because he focused his life on the right priorities.

1. Paul fought the good fight. What is so important that you are willing to fight for it? Are you fighting for your own growth, your relationships, your loved ones, and your witness for Christ?

2. Paul finished the race. It's not how you start the race that matters, it's how you finish it. Who are the people beside you, and what are the disciplines you've put in place to help you finish strong?

3. Paul kept the faith. In the face of unrelenting persecution from both Jews and Gentiles, Paul kept the faith. In spite of intense loneliness, suffering, and long imprisonments, Paul kept the faith. Our faith doesn't stay strong in a vacuum; we need to nurture and exercise it like we do our bodies.

Did Paul have any regrets at the end? Possibly, but compared to the joy and satisfaction he felt as he anticipated hearing his Lord say, "Well done, My good and faithful servant," they paled in comparison.

―――

What are you fighting for right now that's truly worth the effort? What habits do you have in place to keep your pace steady and your faith strong? Do you need to forgive someone or seek reconciliation while there's still time?

Risky Prayer

> At the time of sacrifice, the prophet Elijah stepped forward and prayed: "LORD, the God of Abraham, Isaac and Israel, let it be known today that you are God in Israel and that I am your servant and have done all these things at your command."
>
> 1 Kings 18:36

Several years ago, one of our assistant managers noticed a woman in the checkout line and sensed that God wanted her to pray for this lady, but she felt reluctant. *What if she's offended? What if God really isn't speaking to me about this?* Those questions and others swirled in her mind as she stood there, frozen.

Sometimes God calls His children to take risks, and anytime you are taking a risk for God, you are going to pray! When we're in trouble or when we sense danger, we pray. It's as natural as a young child running into their mother's arms after they fall down on the pavement and skin their knees.

The prophet Elijah found himself in a high-risk, dangerous situation in 1 Kings 18. He confronted the prophets of Baal on Mt. Carmel and proposed a contest to determine who was really God: Baal or the God of Abraham, Isaac, and Jacob. It's a story full of drama, vindication, and judgment through which the Lord God dramatically and definitively asserts His authority and power over false gods.

How did Elijah feel in that moment when he stood before the sacrifice and asked God to act? How would you feel in the face of 450 prophets of Baal who had just been publicly humiliated when their god didn't answer their prayers? He was probably terrified and excited, all at the same time.

So was our assistant manager, as she walked over to the woman and asked if she could have a word of prayer with her. The lady said, "I can't believe you're doing this!" Then she gratefully accepted the prayer offered on her behalf as others nearby stopped to listen. The distressed woman encountered God that day through the risky prayer of one of God's terrified but obedient children, and several bore witness to the power of prayer.

_____

What could risky prayer look like for you this week? Who comes to mind that God wants you to pray for? How might God work in them if you ask to pray for them in person?

Enough Light for the Next Step

Your word is a lamp for my feet, a light on my path.

Psalm 119:105

Sometimes we lose our way. The path that was once level and straight begins taking twists and turns, and we wonder if we are still on the right path after all. Weathering economic downturns, deciding on how to plan for succession, and discerning how to provide our employees' health insurance without violating our conscience were all challenging times when the fog rolled in and obscured our path.

Every Christian has these wilderness experiences. Remember when the Israelites were on their forty-year trek from Egypt to the promised land? That was an extended wilderness experience for an entire nation. God was forming them into His covenant people. God led them through the wilderness by a pillar of cloud and a pillar of fire; when those moved, the people followed. He gave them just enough information to determine their next steps, but no more. Some mornings they looked out of their tents and saw the pillar of cloud was stationary, so they stayed put. Other days the pillar moved, so they packed up and followed it.

The principle is this: in the wilderness, God gives us just enough light for the next step. The Bible paints a picture of this in Psalm 119:105 when it describes God's Word as a "lamp for my feet" and a "light for my path." At night we need a lamp to illuminate a few feet in front of us so we can see and stay on the path. During the day we have the light of the sun, and everything is clear.

But during those dark nights of the soul, when we find ourselves feeling confused and overwhelmed, God's Word still shines the light. Often we only get enough revelation to take the next one or two tentative steps, but God never turns out the lights completely. Even when things seem the darkest, He is always there with us.

———

How has God's Word been a lamp unto your feet during one of your wilderness wanderings? Who do you know that needs a word of encouragement during their dark night of the soul?

DAY 43

Into the Wilderness

> When the dew was gone, thin flakes like frost on the ground appeared on the desert floor. When the Israelites saw it, they said to each other, "What is it?" For they did not know what it was. Moses said to them, "It is the bread the LORD has given you to eat."
>
> Exodus 16:14–15

In our last daily reading, we journeyed with Israel as they traveled to the promised land. Let's stay there a bit longer and see how God provides for His people in the wilderness.

In Exodus 16 we see the first-ever occurrence of manna, God's bread that came down from heaven. An estimated two million people departed Egypt, led by Moses, Miriam, and Aaron. The wilderness they spent decades living in had precious little vegetation or water (think of a mountainous desert region full of rocks). They had no ability to plant crops or gather food but were totally dependent upon God for their survival.

In the morning they were to go out and gather the manna as the sun burned away the dew. God directed them to only gather enough for that day—they were not allowed to gather enough for even two days, except on the day before the Sabbath. If they did, the manna would spoil with maggots, a tough lesson a few of them learned the hard way.

In the wilderness, God often provides just enough sustenance for each day, and no more. Every morning the Israelites gathered God's fresh provision. They literally survived by taking life one day at a time.

The same was true for our family during the financial wilderness of 1985 and 1986. There were days when we honestly didn't know how long we could keep operating. We could only focus on that day. Those were hard months, but God shaped our character and expanded our capacity in the wilderness to prepare us for the day we would enter the good land.

Are you in the wilderness right now financially, relationally, or in some other way? If so, what would it look like for you to pray for God to supply your daily bread and trust that His provision is sufficient for that day?

Water from Rocks

> They camped at Rephidim, but there was no water for the people to drink. So they quarreled with Moses and said, "Give us water to drink." Moses replied, "Why do you quarrel with me? Why do you put the Lord to the test?"
>
> Exodus 17:1–2

Before we move away from Israel in the wilderness, let's pause to consider what we can learn about water, rocks, and honoring God through our leadership.

The first time God miraculously provided water for His people from a rock was in Exodus 17. God directed Moses, their great leader, to strike the rock with his staff, and the water flowed. The second occurrence took place in Numbers 20. This time God again instructed Moses to take his staff, but this time he was to speak to the rock. Instead, Moses vented his frustration with the people of Israel and struck the rock twice. Water again flowed, but God was dishonored.

In fact, God said to Moses and Aaron, "Because you did not trust in me enough to honor me as holy in the sight of the Israelites, you will not bring this community into the land I give them" (Num. 20:12).

This is a sobering reminder for all of us whom God has placed in a position of influence. The greater the authority and sway we've been entrusted with, the higher the standard for our leadership. God disciplines all His children as any good parent would, but He holds leaders more accountable. None of us are exempt.

So, before you set your sights on that corner office, it would be wise to honestly examine your motives. Do you want to look impressive, or do you want to exert godly influence? Do you want to tell other people what to do, or do you want to serve others and set an example of humility?

God exalts the humble and brings down the exalted. Moses, an excellent and godly leader, exalted himself and dishonored God at a critical moment by taking matters into his own hands. We are all tempted to do the same; may God keep our hearts soft and protect us from pride.

Is there a frustrating situation in your life right now where you feel tempted to take matters into your own hands? What insight from Moses's leadership can help you navigate this?

The Lure of Self-Reliance

> There was no one to rescue them because they lived a long way from Sidon and had no relationship with anyone else.
>
> Judges 18:28

I learned many years ago that for Hobby Lobby to thrive, I needed to find good people and let them do their jobs. In fact, I needed to find people who were much better than me in their area and give them both the responsibility and the authority to lead.

One of the great temptations every leader faces is to believe that everything rides on their shoulders alone. We are drawn to this because it appeals to our egos. After all, if the important decisions need to be made by me, I must be pretty smart!

But self-reliance is a trap. Just ask the people of Laish.

Laish was an ancient community of people who lived near the territory the tribe of Dan settled after the death of Joshua. In Judges 18 we discover their fatal flaw: they had no relationship with anyone else. They were alone, self-contained, and self-sufficient. And this made them an easy target for the tribe of Dan, who easily overthrew them and took their cities.

This is a cautionary tale. Don't be like the people of Laish! Don't lead as though everything depends upon you. Don't succumb to the lure and lie of self-reliance. Instead, begin each day acknowledging your complete and utter dependence on God for every good thing in your life—they are all gifts of His grace.

And then invest in the people around you to make them better. Unless they outpace you in their area of leadership, your organization can never realize its potential. Remember, God has given all of us gifts and abilities so that together we can grow up and do the things He calls us to do. Think about it: Jesus never sent a disciple to do anything alone, not even to fetch a donkey.

Are you drawn in by the lure of self-reliance? If so, how has that played out in your leadership? What is something practical you can do this week to invest in the growth of someone else? How can you help to make them better?

A Legacy Worth Leaving

Jesus continued: "There was a man who had two sons. The younger one said to his father, 'Father, give me my share of the estate.' So he divided his property between them."

Luke 15:11–12

What do you want to pass on to your children and grand-children? Barbara and I have discussed and prayed about this question; hopefully you have too. When it comes to what we most want to leave to our three children, their children, and future generations, we decided that money is the easiest to pass down but also the least valuable.

Jesus tells a poignant story in Luke 15 about a father's good legacy that almost gets destroyed because of money. The father was a wealthy man with two sons. The younger son demanded his inheritance early. The father agreed to give it to him, and the young man took off and lived a life of partying and self-indulgence. He blew his inheritance only to end up penniless and hungry.

If the father's legacy was only measured in dollar signs, the first part of the story is not good. The money became a ticket to a wasteful lifestyle. It almost ruined him.

Desperate and humiliated, the son returned home. He prepared to launch into a speech asking for merely a place as a hired hand. But before he could even finish the first sentence, his father called for a new robe for his son, a ring to be placed upon his finger, and a great feast.

What legacy ultimately got passed down? The younger son received:

1. Forgiveness
2. Grace
3. A restored identity as a son
4. The undeserved but much needed delight of a father

What do you really want your legacy to be? If you are only thinking in terms of bank statements and property, I would encourage you to dig deeper. What true riches can you cultivate now that will bless your family later?

———

More so than money and property, what do you most want to pass down to your family? Can you name the top three things you want to leave as your legacy? How does this change the way you are investing today?

Shirtsleeves to Shirtsleeves in Three Generations

An inheritance claimed too soon will not be blessed at the end.

Proverbs 20:21

American industrialist Andrew Carnegie is credited with coining the proverb, "Shirtsleeves to shirtsleeves in three generations." The observed wisdom of this saying goes like this:

- The first generation starts off without wealth. They work hard, seize opportunities, save money, and don't raise their standard of living dramatically. Along the way, they accumulate wealth.

- The second generation "protects" their children from the rigors and sacrifices they had to make, and they focus on providing the best for their family. Their children launch their careers with greater opportunities, exchanging shirtsleeves for blazers and ties. The family wealth plateaus.

- The third generation grows up with all the spoils of wealth. They do not witness their parents making the sacrifices their grandparents made in their shirt-sleeves. They consume the family wealth, seeing it as an entitlement. By the time this generation comes of age, the wealth is gone, and they and their children are back in shirtsleeves.

There is a version of this proverb in almost every country around the world because, sadly, it is a very predictable pattern. In fact, it echoes what we read in Proverbs 20:21 about wealth given to people when they are too young—it won't be blessed in the end!

Will our family be another illustration of this proverb? Will yours?

Of course, we can't control our grandchildren's choices, but we can do a few things to foster a new cycle, one of steward-ship and blessing.

1. Give opportunity, not wealth.
2. Embrace this biblical principle: "The one who is unwill-ing to work shall not eat" (2 Thess. 3:10).
3. Grow a generous vision that is bigger than your family.

Where have you witnessed "shirtsleeves to shirtsleeves in three generations" play out? Which of the three stewardship prin-ciples above do you most resonate with?

A Lost Generation

And all that generation also were gathered to their fathers. And there arose another generation after them who did not know the LORD or the work that he had done for Israel.

Judges 2:10 ESV

An entire generation who did not know the story!

Here's the context. Previously, Abraham had been promised a land and a kingdom in what is now present-day Israel. But Israel had to endure four hundred years of slavery in Egypt. Then, through Moses, God in dramatic fashion (the parting of the Red Sea) brought Israel out of slavery while defeating the Egyptian army. When the time came to finally claim the promised land, the Israelites shrank back, and an entire generation of unbelievers passed away in the wilderness.

Ultimately, God raised up Joshua to bring the nation into the promised land. Following a series of dramatic battles, the tribes of Israel finally took possession of the land.

After the fighting ended, however, it seems the nation got comfortable, complacent, and lazy. They stopped telling the great stories of their slavery in Egypt, how God had set them free, the many struggles along the way, and God's incredible victories.

An entire generation grew up and didn't know the story. Think about it. But we can't blame that generation. We have to blame the generation that stopped telling the story.

It strikes a chord, doesn't it? What stories are you telling your kids and grandkids? Do they know the goodness and power of God's work in your life? Bill High likes to ask, "What are the ten stories your children and grandchildren need to know?"

Why not begin telling those stories now? You could write them down, or record yourself telling them, or simply take the time at special family events to relay how you have personally experienced God's love and grace in your life. The possibilities are endless, but your opportunities to share your God-stories aren't.

———

What are five to ten stories you want preserved for your grandchildren? These stories will reflect how God worked in your life to bring direction, provision, comfort, and blessing to others. How did you come to faith in Christ, and what was it that made the gospel real to you? Have you told that story to your family recently?

Family Wealth

> By wisdom a house is built, and through understanding it is
> established; through knowledge its rooms are filled with rare
> and beautiful treasures.
>
> Proverbs 24:3–4

Family wealth. Those are two big words. When we think about
wealth, we usually think in financial terms. *Financial* wealth
is measured by the numbers. Subtract the liabilities from the
assets, and you come up with the net worth. Or perhaps a different way of saying it is net wealth.

But *family* net worth is less about the numbers and more
about the soft issues. What are the soft issues? They are things
that can't fully be measured by a balance sheet, like the strength
of our relationships and the strength of our communication—
the capital we store in our hearts and minds.

In this equation, family assets look like relational health,
relational equity, family memories, family communication, pro-
ductive family conflict, and family identity. Liabilities look like
unresolved conflict, family secrets, addictive behaviors, isolat-
ing behaviors, and selfishness.

When we look at family assets and liabilities in this way, we can better determine true family net worth. The reality is that growing your family net worth is going to take a lot more effort than padding the investment portfolio every month. It demands three things.

First, it will demand your time. Relationships don't form and strengthen at a distance or over the phone.

Second, it will demand your personal involvement. I make myself available to my family—my children and grandchildren. They can always get on my calendar. That helps communicate that "I am here, I am listening, and I care."

Third, it requires intentionality. In my family, we commit to meeting monthly, quarterly, and annually in different circumstances and settings.

Don't settle for worldly wealth. God has so much more for you! According to Proverbs 24, God wants to fill your home with rare and beautiful treasures.

———

Review the list of family assets and notice which ones are present and which are missing in your family right now. Review the list of liabilities. Which of these do you want to begin paying more attention to?

God's Purpose for Family

> He decreed statutes for Jacob and established the law in Israel, which he commanded our ancestors to teach their children, so the next generation would know them, even the children yet to be born, and they in turn would tell their children. Then they would put their trust in God and would not forget his deeds but would keep his commands.
>
> Psalm 78:5–7

What's the purpose of family? How about companionship, support, or love? These are all good responses. But truly pause and consider, What *is* God's purpose for family?

When we look at the Scriptures, they tell us something profound.

1. Family is the first human institution God established— founded at the creation of the world!

2. God has a generational view of family. God saw from Abraham to Jesus and to the end of the age, all connected through family.

3. Psalm 78 declares God's purpose for the family is to pass on the values taught in Scripture from one

generation to the next—even to the children yet unborn.

Think about it. If a family fulfilled its mission and successfully communicated the values of Scripture from one generation to the next, then our world would be a more beautiful and creative place.

To build this kind of family culture, we must define family values and practices. In the same way a company might define its values as honor, joy, simplicity, creativity, and so on, a family can undertake a similar exercise. Defining family values makes it far easier to define family practices. It also helps to define the *why* of family traditions and activities, whether considering a family vacation, family dinner, or family service project.

But as in any organization, it isn't enough to define those values and practices. The key to building culture is to repeat and reinforce those values, beliefs, and practices day in and day out.

My parents prayed every day, and that value has now been passed on to the fifth generation. What values do you want to outlive you?

What family practices have you established to pass along certain values to the next generation? If you haven't done this yet, where would you like to begin? Which value do you most want to pass down to your grandchildren?

DAY 51

Your Spiritual Family

> While Jesus was still talking to the crowd, his mother and brothers stood outside, wanting to speak to him. . . . "Who is my mother, and who are my brothers?" Pointing to his disciples, he said, "Here are my mother and my brothers. For whoever does the will of my Father in heaven is my brother and sister and mother."
>
> Matthew 12:46–50

We've focused a great deal on the family in these pages. I am blessed that my spiritual family is also my immediate family. Barbara and our three kids are the rock-solid foundation of my life, ministry, and business. But what if you're not married, you don't have children, or your family members are not Christ followers?

Jesus found Himself in this situation early in His ministry. His mother and siblings thought He was out of His mind when they heard the reports about the frenetic pace of His ministry. In fact, we read in Mark 3 they came to the house Jesus was teaching in, apparently to take charge of Him—they didn't believe He was mentally stable. When Jesus was informed that His family was asking for Him, He said His true, spiritual family were those who did God's will. In this instance He made a distinction between His biological family and His spiritual family.

Your flesh and blood family may not join you in serving and obeying God. But that doesn't mean you don't have a family in Christ to walk alongside you. We always seek to honor our parents and show love and grace to our biological families, but God has given us a forever family. None of us are orphans!

Through the consistent witness of Jesus and the love and grace He continued to extend to His family, all or most of them came to faith. His mother, Mary, was with Him at the cross, and His brother James became a leader in the early church and wrote an epistle. Ask God for that same grace with your family as you deepen your connection with your spiritual family.

Who are your spiritual parents and siblings during this season of your life? Who is doing God's will—and helps you to know and follow God's will? How can you prioritize those relationships?

Buried Treasure

> The kingdom of heaven is like treasure hidden in a field. When a man found it, he hid it again, and then in his joy went and sold all he had and bought that field. Again, the kingdom of heaven is like a merchant looking for fine pearls. When he found one of great value, he went away and sold everything he had and bought it.
>
> Matthew 13:44–46

What do you treasure? I love what I do for a living and still go into work on Saturdays, even though most people my age retired long ago. And I love taking care of our employees—it's a privilege and joy to serve them.

But neither my career nor the people I work with are what I treasure most. The most important thing to me is my relationship with Jesus Christ and the honor I have of introducing people to Him. That's my treasure. That's worth selling everything I own to purchase. That's my pearl that gives purpose and joy to my life.

Do you know what your treasure really is? Jesus said if you look into your heart, you will see what you treasure, because where your treasure is your heart will always follow. So, what does your heart tell you? What brings you such excitement that you have trouble going to sleep and can't stop talking about it? What sorrows break your heart, stir something deep inside, and make you want to do something about them? What causes gratitude to bubble up inside of you and overflow as worship?

If you don't know for sure, don't despair. Ask God to help you locate the real treasure of His kingdom. We all get sidetracked by counterfeit treasure—things that are good but not best—from time to time. Ask God to reveal your heart to you and lead you to the pearl of His kingdom; it's there waiting for you to pursue.

Once you find God's treasure, be prepared to let go of the counterfeits, even the ones you have grown so fond of. This is going to cost you, but it's worth infinitely more than whatever you may pay.

———

As you look into the passions of your heart, what do you notice about the things you treasure? What do you find yourself complaining about? What do you find yourself expressing gratitude for?

The Mathematics of the Kingdom

> He told the crowd to sit down on the ground. Then he took the seven loaves and the fish, and when he had given thanks, he broke them and gave them to the disciples, and they in turn to the people. They all ate and were satisfied. Afterward the disciples picked up seven basketfuls of broken pieces that were left over. The number of those who ate was four thousand men, besides women and children.
>
> Matthew 15:35–38

Generosity multiplies. The disciples started with only seven loaves of bread and a few small fish. I'm sure they were skeptical. How could so little feed so many? But after Jesus prayed and they started giving away their little portions, something miraculous began to happen. The loaves and the fish multiplied. They became *more*.

I think, as the disciples watched this miracle, some lessons started to hit home. Generosity begins with gratitude is certainly one lesson. But perhaps the biggest lesson? Start giving away what you have, and start now. I think too many people tell themselves, *When I have more, when I'm a millionaire, then I'll give.* But I'm convinced that unless we give when we have a little, we'll never give when we have a lot.

Stewardship and generosity don't depend on how much you have. They are heart issues.

The people in the churches my dad pastored didn't have much money to tithe with. I'd guess those people would be considered as "working poor" today. But because most of them were farmers, they did have tomatoes, corn, and eggs, so that's what they gave as their tithe. They were demonstrating their trust in God's goodness and provision by stewarding with generosity what they had. And if they were feeling especially generous, our family would end up with a whole chicken!

When you give what you have, no matter how small, in trust and obedience to God as a faithful steward, He will multiply it for His purposes. This is not a give-to-get scheme. It's a get-to-give opportunity. The more God blesses you with, the more you have to give.

Can you recall a time when you gave something that seemed insignificant, but God used it in a big way? If so, be sure to tell someone that story this week.

When Family Hurts

> His brothers then came and threw themselves down before
> him. "We are your slaves," they said. But Joseph said to them,
> "Don't be afraid. Am I in the place of God? You intended to
> harm me, but God intended it for good to accomplish what
> is now being done, the saving of many lives. So then, don't
> be afraid. I will provide for you and your children." And he
> reassured them and spoke kindly to them.
>
> Genesis 50:18–21

Every family experiences friction, tension, and conflict. Parents
can be too harsh or too disengaged, or, worse yet, can be hurt-
ful with their words and actions. Siblings can be jealous of one
another and build up resentments, especially if their parents
display favoritism.

Such was the case with Joseph and his family (see Genesis
37–50). He was his dad's favorite, and everyone knew it, including Joseph. His brothers were angry, and their anger turned
to revenge. They thought about killing him but "spared" him
by selling him into slavery in Egypt.

They then lied to their father and told him Joseph had been
killed by a wild animal. Think of the ripple effect. Joseph suf-

fered as a slave. His father grieved the loss of his son. And his brothers lived with ongoing guilt. There were no innocent bystanders.

Ultimately, after years of living in slavery, Joseph moved past the betrayal and was able to forgive his brothers. How did he do it? Joseph saw the bigger picture of God's work. God was working through Joseph to help save his family and the surrounding nations.

Are there strained relationships in your family? Do you see the ripple effect? Through the life of Joseph, perhaps you can see God's larger plan at work in your family. And perhaps you can see the power of restoration in your family and how it impacts others. We can all learn from Joseph's example and how God always has the bigger picture in mind.

———

When you imagine seeing the members of your family at the next holiday gathering, how does it make you feel? Is there any tension or apprehension? If so, what steps can you take to move toward healing?

The Sorrow of Wealth

> "All these I have kept," the young man said. "What do I still lack?" Jesus answered, "If you want to be perfect, go, sell your possessions and give to the poor, and you will have treasure in heaven. Then come, follow me." When the young man heard this, he went away sad, because he had great wealth.
>
> Matthew 19:20–22

It's a famous story. The rich young ruler sincerely wanted to enter into God's kingdom. He was a good guy. He'd worked at keeping the law. He did good works. But Jesus responded to him in a strange way. He didn't tell him to read the Bible more, go to church more, or to serve more. Jesus told him simply to sell all his possessions, give to the poor, then follow Him. Does that seem harsh? Ruthless, even?

I sometimes wonder what Jesus saw or discerned in this rich young ruler. I'm guessing He sensed there was competition for his heart. Money. Wealth. Possessions. Somewhere along the line, this young man allowed the seeds of worldly affection to take root in his heart. Those roots gave bloom to a disease, and there was only one way to get rid of it: sell everything. Pull out the competitor by the root.

Just a few chapters before, in Matthew 13, Jesus told the parable of the seed and the soil. There, He issued a warning: the worries of this life and the deceitfulness of riches choke God's Word and keep it from bearing fruit.

The rich young ruler walked away sad. As far as we know, this man never came back to Jesus. He couldn't sell his possessions. The roots were too deep. After the young man left, Jesus turned to his disciples and told them, "It is hard for someone who is rich to enter the kingdom of heaven" (Matt. 19:23).

I wish there was a better ending to this story, but there's not. Instead, the story reminds us, challenges us, and calls for us to examine ourselves. What seeds are taking root and blooming in our hearts? If those seeds are anything other than seeds of the kingdom, then we must ruthlessly cultivate the garden. There's too much at stake. Heaven and hell. Life and death. The souls of people.

Take a few minutes and examine the condition of your heart. Is there anything you've allowed to take root there that needs to be eliminated so that you may have "sincere and pure devotion to Christ" (2 Cor. 11:3)?

DAY 56

The Banquet Is Waiting

Then he said to his servants, "The wedding banquet is ready,
but those I invited did not deserve to come. So go to the
street corners and invite to the banquet anyone you find."
So the servants went out into the streets and gathered all
the people they could find, the bad as well as the good, and
the wedding hall was filled with guests.

Matthew 22:8–10

Do you realize that Jesus invites everyone into a relationship
with Him, but many decline the invitation? Jesus told another
compelling story to His disciples, in Matthew 22, that encouraged and alarmed them.

The encouragement was their realization that God wanted
to forgive, restore, and adopt them into His family. To give
them a seat at the banquet table of His grace, love, and joy.

But imagine the alarm they felt when He told them to go
out into the streets and bring in everyone who was willing to
come to this feast, both the good and the bad. Time out! Jesus
wanted to invite "bad" people to His banquet?

Can you imagine sitting at the banquet table next to the bad people? People who lie, steal, live immorally, and disregard God and His Word?

Well, I hope you can, because I just described every single one of us!

The Bible makes it clear that we are all sinners who fall short (Rom. 3:23), and we deserve the penalty of death: eternal separation from God (6:23). We are those people God finds on the street corners and invites to His banquet, even if we grew up going to church every Sunday morning.

You know those "good" people who were invited to the banquet but made excuses? Those are the ones in real danger. What about you? Do you still think that if you are good enough, God will feel compelled to seat you at His banquet table?

You are invited into a relationship with God through Jesus Christ, who is the only way, the only truth, and the only life. Have you humbly accepted His invitation yet?

_____

Have you confessed your sin, brokenness, and inability to ever earn your way into a right relationship with God? Have you invited Jesus into your life as your Savior and Lord? Why not do so today?

Be Humble or Be Humbled

> The greatest among you will be your servant. For those who exalt themselves will be humbled, and those who humble themselves will be exalted.
>
> Matthew 23:11–12

I've had two types of experiences with humility over the years. First, there've been times Barbara and I have humbled ourselves before God by getting on our knees morning, noon, and night, crying out to God for wisdom, provision, and protection. There have also been times when I chose to give the credit for all the success at Hobby Lobby to God and to the people He's blessed us with.

Those have been good moments, blessed times when God was working in my life and shaping my character into someone who looks a bit more like Jesus. And I thank God for each of them.

But there have been other times when I've been humbled. I'm talking now about those painful experiences of unchosen humility that usually follow periods in our lives marked by pride and self-sufficiency.

I have been on my knees begging God for help. Creditors called nonstop, demanding payment with money we didn't have. I had to stand before the family and admit that we could all lose our jobs. The Supreme Court case was an equally challenging time, and the COVID-19 pandemic was another challenge that led to the shutdown of all our stores.

When it comes to humility, it seems we are left with only two choices. We can be humble, or we will be humbled. I think there's nothing God hates more than pride.

Jesus said in Matthew 23 that the greatest among His followers would be a servant. Jesus modeled this for us by taking the role of a servant, even though He is the creator and sustainer of all life. Because He chose to humble Himself, live as a servant, and die a criminal's death on a Roman cross, He has been exalted to the highest place and been given a name that is above all names (Phil. 2:5–11).

Have you experienced times when God exalted you after you chose a path of humility? What do you want to remember this week from those encounters?

DAY 58

Inherited Idolatry

> You shall not make for yourself an image in the form of any-
> thing in heaven above or on the earth beneath or in the waters
> below. You shall not bow down to them or worship them; for I,
> the LORD your God, am a jealous God, punishing the children
> for the sin of the parents to the third and fourth generation
> of those who hate me, but showing love to a thousand gen-
> erations of those who love me and keep my commandments.
>
> Exodus 20:4–6

God wants to be and commands that we honor Him as the most important Person in our lives. He wants to be the object of our affection. An idol is anything that we allow to replace God as the center of our lives. It can be something as blatant as hero worship or something as subtle as our self-indulgent comforts, food, money, power, or receiving applause.

It's the subtle idols that create some of our biggest prob-lems. They may provide temporary satisfaction, but in the end we always need more—more money, more stuff—to be satis-fied. And then, even worse, because these idols are subtle, we can pass our appetites down to our children and grandchildren. They can get used to a similar way of life.

We are warned in Exodus 20 that the sins of the parents are punished down to the third and fourth generations. This means that our children, our grandchildren, and even our great-grandchildren will be impacted by our relationship with God and, conversely, our relationship to idolatry.

You've heard the expression "The apple doesn't fall far from the tree." It's true, isn't it? You don't need to be a psychologist to notice generational patterns of addiction, anger, lust, and workaholism that take their toll on families year after year.

The good news is this: not only is God ready to forgive our idolatry as we confess it and repent but He wants to do so much more. He wants to break the cycle of generational cursing and start a new cycle of generational blessing through you, one that will be passed down to your children's children and, as the verse says, "to a thousand generations."

You see, God loves you right where you're at, warts and all. But He loves you far too much to leave you there!

What form of idolatry did you inherit from your parents? How can you break the generational curses you've inherited and move toward generational blessings?

What Stirs Your Heart?

> Then the whole Israelite community withdrew from Moses's presence, and everyone who was willing and whose heart moved them came and brought an offering to the Lord for the work on the tent of meeting, for all its service, and for the sacred garments.
>
> Exodus 35:20–21

What stirs your heart to live and give generously? Some call it a nudge of the Holy Spirit.

Think about the times you've been nudged. Maybe you saw someone with a broken-down car on the side of the road and stopped to help. Maybe you became aware of an unmet need in your city or church and couldn't sleep that night. Or maybe you saw something in the news about people on the other side of the world whom you would never meet in desperate need of food and shelter, and you knew you must step up in some way.

What can we learn from Exodus 35 and the example of the Israelites who gave generously to the building of the tabernacle? First, they were invited to give: they were made aware of the need and invited to take part in meeting it. Second, they withdrew from Moses and considered their own hearts and the need. I believe that step of considering produced the third step: they were willing. This wasn't coercion.

Their hearts moved them. They felt something inside that compelled them to take action. No doubt this was the Holy Spirit stirring them toward a vision of a new thing God was doing that they got to be a part of. God invited them into His project, not because He needed them but because He wanted to bless them.

Finally, they acted. They brought their offerings. They didn't rationalize away the need. They took action and made the gift.

———

What is stirring your heart right now? What is the vision you are moving toward? What is so important that you must sacrifice other good things so you can pursue it with an undivided heart?

Pull Up the Weeds

Still others, like seed sown among thorns, hear the word; but the worries of this life, the deceitfulness of wealth and the desires for other things come in and choke the word, making it unfruitful.

Mark 4:18–19

I grew up surrounded by farmers, so I learned a few things about growing crops. Of course, you have to start with good seed. Without good seed, everything else you do is for nothing; the life of the plant is bound up in the seed.

But good seed isn't enough. You must also prepare the soil. Farmers do this by plowing and turning the ground, fertilizing, and paying close attention to the amounts of minerals and moisture.

Once the soil is prepared and good seed is sown, the focus shifts to pulling weeds. Weeds are any other plants that compete for the resources your crop needs to thrive. The weeds aren't evil plants, simply different plants taking moisture, sunlight, and nutrients from the plants you're trying to grow.

In Mark 4, Jesus tells a farming story. He describes four different types of soil, three bad and one good. One of the bad soils is full of weeds. These weeds are "the worries of this life, the deceitfulness of wealth and the desires for other things." And just like any weed, they choke the life out of the good seed and make it unfruitful.

Are you worried about what may or may not happen tomorrow? Do you find yourself obsessing over economic or societal trends that evoke fear and uncertainty? Jesus assures us in Matthew 6 that God knows exactly what we need and will provide for us as we seek Him first.

Are you being pulled in by the deceitfulness of wealth? Do you find yourself thinking, *As soon as we get this much in the bank*, or *When my annual earnings surpass this milestone*, or *When we launch that new ministry, store, or division, then I can relax and pay more attention to God and my family*? Jesus asked, "What good is it for someone to gain the whole world, yet forfeit their soul?" (Mark 8:36).

What is competing in your life today with your relationship and love for God? What worries or desires are pulling your mind away from knowing God and trusting Him?

DAY 61

Risk Is Right

Pray also for me, that whenever I speak, words may be given me so that I will fearlessly make known the mystery of the gospel, for which I am an ambassador in chains. Pray that I may declare it fearlessly, as I should.

Ephesians 6:19–20

The apostle Paul took huge risks by openly sharing the message of Christ. And the risk was real. In fact, on several occasions he was beaten and imprisoned. Yet his prayer request to the church in Ephesus was that he would continue to fearlessly make known the gospel. That's courageous!

We all take risks in life. For example, every store we've opened across the country came with risk. The experts tell us that over 65 percent of new businesses fail within ten years. So why would we take the risk to open a new location? Because it's the right thing to do!

Without risk there is no growth.

Without risk there is no learning.

Without risk there is no impact.

As I reflected on this, I was nudged by the Holy Spirit with this question: *You are willing to take risks to grow your business, but are you taking risks for the gospel?*

We live in a culture today where some will take offense to the beliefs and practices of our Christian faith. But we also live in a world filled with people who are thirsty for the living water Jesus offers. The need has never been greater, but the risks are real.

We don't risk beatings and imprisonment in the United States as Paul did, but we do risk rejection, being judged as hateful, and being disregarded as intellectually shallow. And in some cases we risk friendships, our jobs, and maybe our careers.

If risk is right for your business, isn't it right for the gospel? Let's join Paul's prayer that God will give us the courage and compassion to open our mouths and take a risk for the gospel.

Do you remember who first shared the gospel with you? How did God reward them (and you) for taking that risk? Is there a person in your life right now whom you believe God is asking you to share Christ with? How could you take a step forward this week in your witness to them?

The Slavery of Bad Debt

The rich rule over the poor, and the borrower is slave to the lender.

Proverbs 22:7

After God rescued us from our financial crisis in the mid-1980s, I realized that not only was God shaping my character in regard to my pride and self-sufficiency but He was also teaching me something very important about debt.

When you take on long-term debt, it implies you know what the future will bring. But only God knows the future! I was presumptive to think I knew what would happen in the future when we took on our long-term debt. When our business suffered, we weren't able to handle the debt load and keep inventory levels high enough to stay profitable.

We were caught between a rock and a hard place. We were trapped and learned the hard truth of Proverbs 22:7 as our choices became very limited by our lenders.

The first thing we did after getting back into the black was put a plan together to retire our long-term debt and make a commitment to avoid it in the future. It wasn't easy, but through a lot of hard work and the discipline to say no or not yet to a few opportunities, we were able to get rid of all our long-term debt. We were set free!

What did we do with this newfound freedom? We began giving more of our profit away to ministries all over the world. God redirected our debt dollars into the lives of people who needed a tangible expression of His love and an introduction to Jesus Christ. It was one of the best decisions we ever made.

If you are in debt, especially long-term debt that stretches into the distant future, I encourage you to pray for God's direction. Who knows, maybe He will lead you to retire that debt and free up those dollars for something that has eternal value.

When you think about your current debt load, how does it make you feel? Are you prayerful about your relationship with debt as a steward of God's resources? What difference would it make if you got rid of your long-term debt?

Divine Appointments

When Jesus reached the spot, he looked up and said to him, "Zacchaeus, come down immediately. I must stay at your house today."

Luke 19:5

In 2014 our family experienced one of the hardest trials we've ever faced when we reluctantly took the US government to court. We believe that individuals do not lose their religious freedom when opening a family business—yet we were legally required to provide potentially life-terminating drugs and devices through our insurance plan. Our case ended up going before the Supreme Court.

While in DC for the hearing, our general counsel, Peter Dobelbower, got in a cab to tour the city with his wife. At the end of the ride the Nigerian cab driver handed him a card that asked, "Do you know Jesus?" Peter, a man of deep faith, said he did. He went on to ask the driver to pray for him as he defended our case.

But the driver cut him off and said, "Yes, I know who you are. This is your divine appointment, and you will win."

God sent a total stranger to Peter at a moment he desperately needed to hear from God. We see this happening to Zacchaeus in Luke 19 as Jesus walks by, looks up at him, and says He wants to stay in his home. Zacchaeus put himself in Jesus's path, and in a way no one could have predicted, it became his divine appointment.

As you ask God to go before you and give you the wisdom to know and do His will, keep your eyes open for divine appointments. Often they come in the form of interruptions, something that was not on your to-do list for the day. Sometimes God sends you to another person you may not even know with a message you need to hear, and sometimes God sends you unexpected people.

God is alive, and He speaks to us through His Word and also through these unplanned encounters. If we pay attention and remain open, we may catch a glimpse of Jesus walking by.

Have you ever experienced a divine appointment? Looking back on it, have you ever missed a divine appointment because you were too busy and failed to recognize it? How can you be more open to God speaking to you—and through you—this week?

Your True North

In their hearts humans plan their course, but the LORD estab-
lishes their steps.

Proverbs 16:9

Debbie Kinsey, our director of management ministries, tells
a story about how God turned around the life of one of our
comanagers. He was part of a meeting where small gifts were
distributed to encourage the team. He happened to receive
a compass, and at first felt sorry for himself because several
others received nicer gifts.

As he walked across the parking lot on his way to work the
next day, he reached his hand into his coat pocket and felt the
compass. In that moment God spoke powerfully to him, saying,
*You are going in the wrong direction, and I'm here to tell you
that you need to have Me in your life.* He gave his life to God
right in that parking lot!

We all need a compass. We need a true north. We all need
the voice of the Holy Spirit redirecting our lives to God.

Like sheep without a shepherd, we so easily go astray and
miss out on the blessings and growth God wants for us. Prov-

erbs 16:9 reminds us that in our hearts we can plan our course, but only God can establish our steps as He directs us toward the abundant life Christ came to give us.

So as you make plans for your family, your business, and your ministry, remember that your plans are at best educated guesses. We all need to make the best plans we can by praying about them and seeking good advice, but also we must hold them loosely. The most important question to ask ourselves isn't *What have I planned?* but *What is God establishing?*

As you begin to see the good but often surprising things God is establishing in your life, you get aligned with what God is doing and the direction He's heading. Like Henry Blackaby said, "Watch to see where God is working and join Him in His work."*

You will have your own parking lot encounters with the Holy Spirit. When God speaks to your heart, be prepared to change your direction.

How has God changed your plans lately? Can you recall a time God redirected you away from something you planned to something else that, in the end, was far better?

* Henry T. Blackaby and Claude V. King, *Experiencing God: How to Live the Full Adventure of Knowing and Doing the Will of God* (Nashville: Broadman & Holman, 1994).

Listen to Your People

Moses' father-in-law replied, "What you are doing is not good. You and these people who come to you will only wear yourselves out. The work is too heavy for you; you cannot handle it alone."

Exodus 18:17–18

Business consultants talk a lot about how important it is to hire people smarter than we are. While I consider that excellent advice, I do wonder, If we are hiring such smart people, why don't we listen to them?

Too often those of us with important titles and more experience just assume we have the best ideas. So when a younger or less experienced person offers an observation or makes a suggestion, we can easily dismiss them. And, in doing so, we often miss two important opportunities:

1. We can miss the game-changing wisdom of their ideas.

2. We can miss the opportunity to grow our younger or less experienced leaders by taking what they have

to say seriously and deferring to them whenever practical.

Moses faced this exact situation. One day his father-in-law, Jethro, was visiting, and he observed Moses hard at work. Later, he pulled Moses aside and made an important observation, followed by a recommendation: "You are going to burn out! You need to delegate the workload to more people."

Moses could have ignored his father-in-law. After all, God had put Moses in charge! But rather than dismissing this unrequested but needed input, he was honest and humble enough to see the wisdom in it. He received Jethro's observation and implemented his advice. Moses was a secure enough leader not to feel threatened by championing someone else's good idea.

Do you remember how it felt in the early days of your career when someone important listened to what you had to say and took it to heart? You probably felt respected and competent. Your idea may not have been fully formed yet, but when leaders really listened and actually did something with one of your ideas, you began to see yourself as a capable leader.

One more thing: you don't have to wait around hoping for people to share their ideas. You can ask them. Try it!

———

Who could you encourage and invest in this week? What questions can you ask to get them talking about their ideas? Here's one you can try: "How do you think we can move forward with this?"

The Problem with Perfect

> Then Caleb silenced the people before Moses and said, "We should go up and take possession of the land, for we can certainly do it."
>
> Numbers 13:30

Have you ever worked with someone who always felt like they needed more information before they could make a decision? Or have you ever been ready to move forward with a plan only to see it languish because the person in charge was waiting for the perfect conditions?

I've always been one of those people who wants to take action, to do something (even if it turns out to be the wrong thing). I'm grateful for those people God has placed in my life to slow me down at times, but I would still rather try to do something than wait indefinitely.

I love what Caleb said in Numbers 13 when he returned with the eleven others who were sent by Moses to spy out the land. His report can be summed up as, "The land is good, God is with us, let's go!"

Caleb was a man of action who didn't allow perfectionism to stall him out and leave him stuck in inactivity. How was he able to boldly step out and take action? For starters, we know from the Bible that he trusted God and put his confidence in God's Word. Fear, not faith, tends to drive perfectionism. Caleb's faith was strong, which helped keep his fear in check.

He also relied upon what he'd learned about God through his personal experience. He saw the Red Sea part, he drank the water that came from the rock, and he tasted the manna from heaven. He knew God personally and had his own experiences walking with God.

If you struggle to take action for fear of making a mistake because everything isn't perfect enough to get started, learn from Caleb. Get maximum clarity on what God is saying to you, find at least one other person who shares your faith and desires to do whatever God is asking (Caleb had Joshua), and bring to memory and talk about your personal experiences with God and what you learned through them.

Where do you tend to get stuck with perfectionism? What are you afraid of in those moments? What could happen if you shared those fears with someone and prayed for increased faith?

Clean Hands and a Pure Heart

> Who may ascend the mountain of the LORD? Who may stand in his holy place? The one who has clean hands and a pure heart, who does not trust in an idol or swear by a false god.
>
> Psalm 24:3–4

Sitting in my hotel room during a business trip to Asia, I found myself in the middle of a divine appointment. As our lower-than-expected profit reports were being faxed to me, the Holy Spirit met with me through Psalm 24. God's message was simply this: *Walking with integrity, with clean hands and a pure heart, is far more important than running a successful business.*

That was over forty years ago, but the power of that encounter carries me to this day. Like every business owner, I want to run a profitable business, and that desire for profit can tempt me to take shortcuts—to fudge here and there, resulting in a loss of integrity.

We've all heard the sad stories of extremely successful business and ministry leaders who were brought down because they didn't have clean hands or a pure heart. In one way or another, these world-class leaders succumbed to placing profit, fame, or maybe even control above their integrity. They lied, cheated, and stole because they believed at some level the risks were worth it.

What happened to them? The insight from Psalm 24 suggests they trusted in an idol, a false god. Let's just call it the god of success. We serve this idol every time we place our professional success above our success at home. We bow to this false god whenever we set aside our faithfulness to Christ to get ahead and win against our competitors.

Concerned about the cleanliness of your hands or the purity of your heart? I have good news: the Bible says in 1 John 1:9 that if we confess our sins, God will forgive and purify us. It's only when we choose to hide our sins rather than confess them that we get into real trouble. So confess your sin to God and to a respected Christian friend, and trust God will lead you with pure hands and a clean heart.

———

Do you have someone you trust enough to confess your sins to? If not, how can you cultivate that kind of friendship?

Give Up Ownership

> Go, sell everything you have and give to the poor, and you will have treasure in heaven.
>
> Mark 10:21

I was one of those guys who always said, "God is the owner of everything!" But I've found it's a lot easier to say that than to do something about it.

On paper, I owned 85 percent of the stock of Hobby Lobby, and my children owned the other 15 percent. Legally and practically, I was the owner along with my family. In theory, I could do whatever I wanted—sell it, mortgage it, take all the profits for myself. To make God the owner meant that I'd have to give up my voting rights, and so would my children and their adult children.

That's what we did. We signed away our rights and made God the owner. To some, that might not make much sense, but by signing away our rights we experienced relief and freedom. I always said that if I lost one child because of the wealth of Hobby Lobby, it would be better if our company never existed. I saw that what we had could impact future generations to come—great-grandchildren I'd never meet.

But when we signed away our right of ownership, we also took on a different responsibility. We were stewards of what God put in our hands. We were accountable to take care of what He'd given us. How we used what we'd been given mattered.

Maybe you are like me. You may say that God is the owner of everything, but do you treat what you have as if *you* are the owner? You don't have to be the owner of a company. It may be your house, your apartment, your car, your clothes. And if you do own a business, are you willing to give up your stock?

Ownership is about the right to control. Stewardship is about the responsibility to manage.

———

As you consider all God has put in your hands, do you consider yourself the owner—the one entitled to the benefit of those things? Are you willing to make God the owner of all you have, with the responsibility of being a steward?

Structure Matters

He must manage his own family well.

1 Timothy 3:4

In the organizations I'm part of, there are necessary structures to make things work. We have officers, directors, regional managers, district managers, store managers—you get the picture. We have regular meetings of our leadership team that help keep us on the same page about how we are operating and how we may need to make adjustments and changes. We have meetings to inspire us and remind us of our purpose.

In our families, we tend to not operate with any similar structure.

Perhaps Sundays are a time for worship, but the rest of the week is ruled by activities. We allow the activity schedules to govern our family: sports schedules, academic schedules, school calendars. They dictate when and where we gather. In a similar way, we tend to let places like church, school, and athletic clubs drive the character development and spiritual training of our children. Is it any wonder we end up with results we don't like?

My family doesn't claim to be perfect, but one of the things we've learned to prioritize is meeting regularly as a family. When our kids were growing up, we worked hard to gather around the dinner table regularly. And as they got older, we had family meetings built around the business but also a monthly meeting to discuss our giving. We found giving was a great place to have discussions built around our values.

One of the things we added in later years, as our family expanded, was a monthly or quarterly meeting to celebrate birthdays and affirm one another. We also have an annual family celebration where we remind ourselves of our family vision, mission, and values.

All these ideas reflect practices we see in the Bible. For instance, Sabbath is a practice that occurs weekly. And there are annual festivals, such as Passover, that provide a place of rest and also a time to remember what God has done in our lives. These regular occurrences provide structure for our family to gather, remember, and thrive.

Have you implemented a structure for your family, a regular schedule for meetings to rest, remember, and celebrate? What additions might you make? Or are you allowing activities to direct your schedule instead of you? Are there some you should consider eliminating?

Vision, Mission, and Values

Write the vision; make it plain on tablets, so he may run who reads it.

Habakkuk 2:2 ESV

One of the things I'll often say in front of groups about my coauthor Bill is that he helps families with legacy. I think a lot of people associate the idea of legacy with creating a legal document like a will or a trust, or sometimes you'll hear the phrase "leave a legacy" in terms of wealth management.

But I think legacy is a lot more about teaching values and virtues to your children. The plan is that they will in turn teach those values to their children, who will teach their children—for generations! Legacy is more about what you instill inside of a person's heart that can be carried into the future.

For our family, with Bill's help, we came together to work on defining our vision, mission, and values. It wasn't so much that we didn't have good ideas of what we believed, but we'd never taken the time to write them down.

We'd previously written the vision, mission, and values for our business, and those statements helped guide our business on a day-to-day basis. But it had never occurred to us that we should do something similar for our family. In fact, when we get our comanagers together three to five times per year, I'll often say to them that it is far easier to be successful at business than it is to be successful at family.

Today, we've got our vision, mission, and values displayed on a color document my daughter designed. Every family member has a copy, and we do an annual celebration where we remind ourselves of the ideas that guide our family.

When I was first married, I had three simple goals: to have a great marriage, to have children who would serve God, and to be successful in my career. Now, as I contemplate our vision, mission, and values, I've added two more goals: to have grandchildren and great-grandchildren—generations—who will also serve God, and to tell as many people as I can about the person of Jesus who loves them.

When you consider Habakkuk 2:2, how does the written clarity of a vision statement allow someone to run and thrive? How can your family implement its own vision, mission, and values statement?

Live Out Your Code

And these words that I command you today shall be on your heart. You shall teach them diligently to your children.

Deuteronomy 6:6–7 ESV

Sometimes I think the Old Testament gets a bad rap. Admittedly, it's easy to get lost with all the genealogies, tribes, lands, and back-and-forth. But my son Steve reminds me the Bible is really all one story: a story of how a loving God wants to restore everyone to relationship with Him.

In the same way, the Old Testament talks about living by the law. There are a lot of laws—hundreds of them. But I think the idea is simpler than we make it out to be. We can overcomplicate things. Instead, I think of it as living by a code. The Lord wanted His children to put Him first, to love Him and honor Him. And then He wanted them to love their neighbors, the people around them.

Jesus summed up the law in that way, into that code (Matt. 22:37–40). This is the way of life.

Once we have our code, we are to repeat it, repeat it, repeat it. That's really the idea of Deuteronomy 6:6–7. We should live out the Bible's code day by day. We talk about it when we get up, when we go to bed, and whenever we are walking around—pretty much all the time.

We've tried to live that out in our business and in our family. We never want to overcomplicate things. We want to keep the main thing the main thing. In business, we buy and sell merchandise. That's our main thing. If we get away from that idea, we can start doing things like running a restaurant inside of Hobby Lobby.

In our family, we want to keep the main thing the main thing too. We want to love God intimately, and we want to tell as many people as we can about Jesus. Sometimes we say that we are about God's Word and people's souls. Keeping it simple in our family helps us stay focused, and it helps our children, grandchildren, and great-grandchildren carry on in the same way.

What are the ideas—the code—inside your family and business that should be repeated again and again? What are ways you pass these ideas on to the next generation of leaders and family members?

Give 50 Percent?

> Give, and it will be given to you. A good measure, pressed down, shaken together and running over, will be poured into your lap. For with the measure you use, it will be measured to you.
>
> Luke 6:38

At least a few times per year, Bill and I host events with business leaders from around the country. One of the things people always want to talk about is generosity.

Some have heard that our family gives away 50 percent of the profits of our company. Usually when that topic comes up, Bill will stop and ask me, "Why give 50 percent?" He makes the point that it would be easy to rationalize investing more, saving more, or even buying some things that I or the family might want.

Over the years, I've had different answers to his question. But, ultimately, I've settled on one answer. I tell the story of my mother, Marie. When she died, she passed away in the arms of her daughter. As she was passing, she cried out, "Do you see them? Do you see them?" It was angels coming to take my mother to her heavenly home.

My mother wasn't wealthy in a worldly sense. In the eyes of the world, she was a nobody, but in God's economy, she was important enough to send angels to bring her home. Any billionaire would be willing to trade places with my mother.

What was her secret? My mother was content. She didn't need more stuff, more clothes, more cars, more homes, more savings. She had enough. She was focused not on this life but on the life to come—her heavenly home.

Why give 50 percent? Because I don't need any more of this world's goods, but I want to do all that's in my power to bring others to experience God's love. So perhaps a better question might be "Why *not* give 50 percent?" Why wouldn't I give more for those things that will last? Why would I keep more for myself when it will only be consumed?

I'm reminded of the C. T. Studd poem my mom kept on the wall of our home: "Only one life, 'twill soon be past, only what's done for Christ will last."

As you consider your own giving and generosity, is there another percentage you should consider—perhaps over and above the tithe?

Good to Better?

> What good will it be for someone to gain the whole world,
> yet forfeit their soul? Or what can anyone give in exchange
> for their soul?
>
> Matthew 16:26

Jim Collins wrote *Good to Great*, a very influential book, back in 2001. It's a helpful, well-researched book that tracks the success of companies as measured by longevity and stock value. But I have to ask, Is high stock price really the chief measure of success? I would suggest a more fitting title would be *Good to Better*.

Why? Because in my view, no company can become truly great unless it focuses on eternity.

One of the ways we've tried to focus on the eternal is by reminding ourselves often that the real bottom line of Hobby Lobby is caring deeply for the souls of our employees. God has entrusted tens of thousands of people to our care; how are we stewarding that responsibility?

Jesus asked a powerful question in Matthew 16 that helps bring clarity to this conversation: "What good will it be for someone to gain the whole world, yet forfeit their soul?" That question should give you pause as you consider your goals for the coming year. Ask yourself:

- What good will it be to die a billionaire if your children and grandchildren don't love and serve God?
- What good will it be to double your profit margin if your employees feel used and unimportant?
- What good will it be to ascend to the corner office if your marriage suffers and the two of you drift apart?
- What good will it be to grow your business through practices that sacrifice your integrity and undermine your witness for Christ?

So, do you want to aim for "good to better" or "good to great"?

In what ways are you focusing on eternity right now in your organization? What might you do over the next three months to increase your focus on the eternal?

Ask Jesus to Direct Your Business

> When he had finished speaking, he said to Simon, "Put out into deep water, and let down the nets for a catch." Simon answered, "Master, we've worked hard all night and haven't caught anything. But because you say so, I will let down the nets."
>
> Luke 5:4–5

Jesus's profession before starting His public ministry was building things. Most of us grew up thinking of Him as a carpenter, but more likely He was a stonemason, because wood was such a limited resource. In either event, He built things using available materials, and He was probably very good at it.

I am a merchandiser. You may be a computer programmer, a ministry leader, a student, or a full-time parent devoted to raising your family. Some of you may also be builders, like Jesus was. But whatever you do, Jesus understands it and can be trusted to direct the big and little decisions you make for your business.

Not only was Jesus the best, smartest, and most capable spiritual leader who ever lived but He was also the best, smartest, and most capable business leader. Think about it: by recruiting and training a small group of leaders, He started an organization called the church that literally turned the world upside down and continues to do so over two thousand years after its launch.

Jesus demonstrated His business intelligence in a dramatic way in Luke 5 by advising Peter and his fishing crew. They had been fishing all night and caught nothing. Jesus sent them back out at the "wrong time" of day to try it again—and they caught so many fish their boats almost capsized!

Jesus's wisdom so often flies in the face of everything worldly authorities tell us. The world says, "If you want to be a leader, use people to get ahead." Jesus says, "If you want to be a leader, humble yourself by serving people."

So, as you think about going to work on Monday morning, what decisions do you need to make that Jesus can speak into? Remember, He cares about the little things and the big things. Nothing is too insignificant to bring to Him in prayer.

What upcoming decisions do you want to ask Jesus to give you direction on? What "small" things do you want to start praying about this week?

DAY 75

Anti-Retirement Planning

Now then, just as the Lord promised, he has kept me alive for forty-five years since the time he said this to Moses, while Israel moved about in the wilderness. So here I am today, eighty-five years old! I am still as strong today as the day Moses sent me out; I'm just as vigorous to go out to battle now as I was then.

Joshua 14:10–11

The average American retires at age sixty-five. I guess that makes me quite the oddity! As I've mentioned, I'm over eighty years old and still go to work five days a week, plus most Saturdays.

The idea of retirement our culture embraces—not working, moving someplace warm, playing golf, filling your time watching TV, and taking it easy—simply isn't biblical. I can appreciate its appeal on some days when I'm feeling tired or discouraged, but I believe God wants so much more for us in our golden years.

Take Caleb, for example. In Joshua 14, Caleb, then eighty-five years old, asks Joshua's permission to take the mountainous territory Moses promised to him forty-five years earlier.

Caleb is still strong physically and mentally, and instead of coasting into a life of ease, he wants to engage new opportunities and fight new battles.

How are you thinking about retirement? Whether you're already retired or just contemplating it, I encourage you to give prayerful consideration to these questions:

1. What wisdom have you gained that God wants you to share with others?
2. What skills have you learned that need to be passed down to younger generations?
3. What gets you out of bed in the morning? What are you so passionate about that you would devote time and energy to it without getting a paycheck?

We may not be as strong physically as Caleb was when we are eighty-five, but we have so much more to offer than our physical strength. God has deposited His grace and truth into our lives over the decades, and He still has something important for us to do even into our eighties.

How do you view retirement? What do you appreciate about Caleb's example? How does this challenge you to think and plan differently?

Succession God's Way

> So the LORD said to Moses, "Take Joshua son of Nun, a man in whom is the spirit of leadership, and lay your hand on him."
>
> Numbers 27:18

Who will take over for you when God calls you home or reassigns you? This is a question I have given a lot of thought to in recent years. I've been leading Hobby Lobby for over fifty years, but I won't be leading it for the next fifty years. Someone will take my place. None of us are indispensable to God.

At the advanced age of 120, Moses was called home by God. He'd led the nation of Israel for forty years, but the day came when he had to turn over the privilege and responsibility of leadership to someone else.

It appears Moses was conflicted over God's plan for succession. On the one hand, Moses had a great deal of confidence in the new leader, Joshua. But on the other hand, Moses wanted to keep leading a little longer and cross the Jordan with the people to enter the land God had promised them. This must have been a bittersweet experience for Moses, and indeed, that's how most of us will feel when we hand over the baton of leadership.

What can we learn from Moses's example? For one thing, we can start investing early in other leaders by including them in what we do. Moses consistently had Joshua at his side when he met with God, made crucial decisions, and communicated with the elders.

We can also learn to bless and release the next generation of leaders. God told Moses to "lay your hand on him." This was a public way Moses acknowledged Joshua as the new leader and basically said to the people, "As you have followed me, now I want you to follow Joshua."

Finally, we learn that letting go of leadership is hard. Don't expect this to be an easy experience! Too many leaders hold on to the reins for too long and inadvertently hurt their organizations. Just as God was able to use you as a leader, with all your shortcomings, so He is able to use a new leader. Remember, you are a steward; and God is the owner!

_____

What aspect of Moses's example do you want to follow going forward? How are you including developing leaders in what you do?

Why You Need to Tell Your Story

The man from whom the demons had gone out begged to go with him, but Jesus sent him away, saying, "Return home and tell how much God has done for you." So the man went away and told all over town how much Jesus had done for him.

Luke 8:38–39

You have a story to tell. Your life, with all its ups and downs, tells a story people need to hear. Some of us dismiss our stories because we don't have a formal Bible education or because we're embarrassed about something we may have said or done. I hesitated at one time to tell my story because I didn't go into vocational ministry. I grew up in a home that gave special honor to pastors and missionaries, and rightly so, but I went into business. Why would people want to hear my story?

Jesus helps us understand the power our stories hold by the way He responds to a dangerous man in Luke 8. We are never given the man's name, only the name the demons who possessed him told Jesus: Legion. He was violent, a danger to himself and others, and so strong not even chains could hold him down.

Jesus confronted and cast out the demons who'd tormented him and revealed Himself as the Son of God. Once in his right mind, the man asked Jesus if he could follow Him as one of His disciples. But Jesus said no, because He had something better in mind. He told this new believer to go back home and tell everyone how much God had done for him.

You see, it would be one thing for you or me to meet this man today and hear the amazing story about the way Jesus transformed his life. But it would be far more powerful if we really knew him, if we grew up with him and saw his life spiral out of control and then reunited with him after Jesus had healed and restored him.

Remember, your story points to Jesus, and that's what people need most.

———

What parts of your story can you begin sharing with people? Have you told your children and grandchildren passages of your story that could point them to Christ?

The Real Mission of Business

> After this, Paul left Athens and went to Corinth. There he met a Jew named Aquila . . . [and] his wife Priscilla. . . . Paul went to see them, and because he was a tentmaker as they were, he stayed and worked with them.
>
> Acts 18:1–3

When people hear my life story and how God has blessed our family and Hobby Lobby so abundantly for so many years, they often seem most impressed by these numbers:

- We went from $150 in sales to $8 billion annually in fifty years.
- We employ over fifty thousand people.
- We operate over one thousand stores across the country.

Yes, those are big numbers! And yes, I am grateful for the grace and generosity of God—our growth is only because of Him. But there's another number that I think is far more important: we give 50 percent of our profits to charitable causes that point people to God's Word and a personal relationship with Jesus Christ.

You can grow a big company even if you don't acknowledge God's blessing, but you will never lead a great company unless you focus on the eternal. Selling merchandise is what we do, and with God's help, we've been successful. But demonstrating and sharing the good news of Jesus Christ with people whom God loves so much He sent His Son to die for is our real mission.

We read in Acts 18 that Paul, upon arriving in Corinth, ran a small business. He was a tentmaker. He worked with his hands to manufacture and sell a commodity people needed and were willing to pay for. Through his business he supported himself and those who served with him. But his mission in life wasn't making tents, it was making disciples!

You may be a butcher, a baker, or a candlestick maker—it doesn't make any difference. Your business is a means to support yourself, your family, and your employees, and it is a platform for the gospel. How you care for your staff and customers, your integrity, and your good stewardship of God's resources gives you the opportunity to demonstrate and talk about the gospel.

———

How can your business vision incorporate God's ultimate vision? Do you pay as close attention to the spiritual impact you are making as you do your profit margin?

It All Starts at Home

> But you will receive power when the Holy Spirit comes on
> you; and you will be my witnesses in Jerusalem, and in all
> Judea and Samaria, and to the ends of the earth.
>
> Acts 1:8

Do you have a giving strategy?

We call Oklahoma City home. We live here, our headquarters are here, and we worship and shop here. In fact, forty-four members of the extended Green family live in the Oklahoma City metropolitan area.

Discussing this one day, our son Mart commented, "We can do ministry in other places and help there, but we don't live there. People don't know us there. As we get closer to our own city, we have the potential to have more impact."

Jesus started an international ministry not by going out to the nations but by staying home. Much of His ministry took place in Galilee, which was near His hometown of Nazareth. In His parting words to His disciples, He gives them a ministry model: Jerusalem, Judea, Samaria, and the ends of the earth.

I think that's a good model. Consider what you can do in your own city, then regionally, then the surrounding regions, then the nations. There's little doubt that we believe in getting the gospel out to the entire world. But I've also seen others focus so much on the rest of the world they forget their hometown. Mart has helped me see that. Wrestling with this balance of giving to the nations versus giving locally is a healthy thing.

Giving locally starts with investing in your local church and can also extend to helping the poor and needy in your community, the prisoners, and the widows. These are all areas we can touch and give to individually.

But Mart also talks about the idea of "collective impact." How do we solve problems bigger than any one organization or person? For instance, the homeless issue in our community is bigger than any one organization. The trafficking issue is bigger than any one organization. Sometimes our giving and our ministry can extend to bringing multiple people and multiple organizations together to address the big issues of our day.

Let's follow Jesus's command to be His witnesses locally, regionally, globally—and strategically!

———

Sometimes we overlook the people right in front of us. Pray today for fresh eyes of faith to see the mission field you already live in. What opportunities for you to share God's love are literally just around the corner?

DAY 80

Gray Hair Required

> Since my youth, God, you have taught me, and to this day I
> declare your marvelous deeds. Even when I am old and gray,
> do not forsake me, my God, till I declare your power to the
> next generation, your mighty acts to all who are to come.
>
> Psalm 71:17–18

My hair turned gray several years ago. Most of us don't like the thought of getting older because we live in a culture that worships youth. Just think about the ads we see every day. "Staying young" is big business, but according to Psalm 71 it misses an important point.

We should challenge the idea that advancing age moves us to retirement homes and golf courses. Our culture promotes the idea that gray hair gives us less of a seat at the table, but the psalmist says just the opposite. We are to declare—loudly, boldly, emphatically—God's marvelous deeds. The power of gray hair is that it means we've seen a lot. We've done a lot. We've witnessed the different ways God has shown up in our lives. We've seen God's deliverance time and time again. We've known His marvelous deeds!

The idea of declaration is so important that it's repeated in the psalm. In addition to declaring God's deeds, we declare His power. We speak of the character of God. We speak of His rule and His reign. We speak of His reach. There's nothing He cannot touch. There's nothing hidden from Him. The rulers of nations submit to Him.

Who are these declarations directed to? The next generation and all to come. The Lord wants us to be a voice of declaration to our children and our grandchildren. But our family is not our limit. Our declarations are for *all* who are to come.

Our job is to tell the story of all God has done, of His incredible power and majesty. I know that sometimes we think our kids don't want to hear the stories. But in the final season of our lives, this side of heaven, our job is to tell those stories. These are stories about our personal experiences with God: how He came through for us when all hope was lost, how He brought healing and health back into our lives and relationships, and how He set us free from the bondage of sin.

We need the grayheads among us to put aside their coast into retirement and instead declare God's marvelous deeds and power.

———

What important experiences with God do you want to pass down to younger generations? What is God teaching you now that you will carry for the rest of your life?

Trouble Is Coming

I have told you these things, so that in me you may have peace. In this world you will have trouble. But take heart! I have overcome the world.

John 16:33

Have you ever read a book or listened to a sermon that basically said, "If you trust Jesus, life will be easy! God wants you to be happy all the time"? While these "Happily ever after" messages feel good, they don't square up with what Jesus tells us in John 16.

As Jesus prepared His disciples for His departure, He shot straight with them. He told them this world system (under the influence of the evil one) would resist and reject them. In other words: "Get ready; trouble is coming."

But He didn't stop there. He went on to say, "Take heart! I have overcome the world." Jesus wanted them to know that hard times and suffering awaited them, but they shouldn't be dismayed or discouraged by that reality, because He would be with them. And having Jesus with them meant the One who faced the worst the devil and this world could throw at

Him, yet overcame it all, would get them through the troubles to come.

Our family has known financial troubles, legal troubles that took us all the way to the Supreme Court, and all the turmoil and heartache caused by the 2020 pandemic. God didn't spare us from these difficult times, but He did walk with us through them. And when you know God is with you in troubling times, you can experience the peace only Jesus can give.

In fact, it's the peace of Jesus we experience in the midst of the storms of life that shines a bright light into the darkness. Others are going through similar heartaches, and when they see the peace we have, it will point them toward Jesus.

When have you experienced a troubling time that brought suffering and hardship but also an awareness of Jesus's presence that brought deep peace? What did you learn from that? How can you stay sufficiently connected with Jesus and a faith community to receive the peace He offers when trouble comes your way?

The Painful Gift

> Do not rebuke mockers or they will hate you; rebuke the wise
> and they will love you. Instruct the wise and they will be wiser
> still; teach the righteous and they will add to their learning.
>
> Proverbs 9:8–9

Rebuke—what does that mean? We don't hear that word a lot
these days. A rebuke is a strong criticism or a challenge to actions or attitude.

I grew up in the South, where whatever the boss says, goes.
You didn't challenge your boss. I learned to keep quiet and
do what I was told. And while that experience taught me to
honor authority, it didn't prepare me to lead.

As a young leader, I brought some of that same authori-
tarian style to the table. I was more focused on the goal than
on listening. I was less open to rebuke or challenge. After all,
I was the boss.

I soon realized that if our managers adopted that same
style of leadership, it would kill our business. We would squash
all our people's good ideas. I needed to open myself up to
the ideas and input of others, even if they challenged me.

The truth of Proverbs 9 hit home: rebuke the wise, and they will love you.

Those who are wise accept rebuke. They accept challenge. They appreciate when someone cares enough to speak up and turn them from a bad path. The truth is that sometimes we need those stronger words to shake some sense into us. In fact, the wise respond with love and appreciation to those who provide that rebuke.

On the other hand, those who reject rebuke are called mockers. Mockers make the person who offers the rebuke feel bad for speaking up. That's why the verse says mockers "hate you." They'd rather run off a cliff than receive instruction. That's foolish.

Are you willing to accept a good rebuke, a challenge to your leadership? Do you promote an environment of good and honest challenge? Or is there mockery—do you make fun of those who provide that challenge?

These are hard words, a rebuke, but to the wise it's a good gift from God. Those who challenge us and pull us back from taking a wrong way truly love us.

———

Do people in your organization feel comfortable telling you the truth and offering their ideas? How often do others disagree with you and share their ideas? How can you invite more feedback from your team while making people feel more safe to share openly?

Don't Be the Elephant in the Room

> Jesus called them together and said, "You know that the rulers of the Gentiles lord it over them, and their high officials exercise authority over them. Not so with you. Instead, whoever wants to become great among you must be your servant."
>
> Matthew 20:25–26

Have you ever been the elephant in the room? Do others view you as so big and important that your opinion trumps everyone else's? Do conversations stop when you enter a room and resume after you leave?

I confess that, as founder and CEO of Hobby Lobby, I have been the elephant in the room on too many occasions. But I don't want to be the elephant, and you shouldn't either. Why? Because no one person is smart enough to get it right every time. There's no individual leader, no matter how gifted, who possesses all the gifts and talents required to grow and lead a successful organization.

We need to reassess our view of leadership by taking Jesus's words in Matthew 20 more seriously. When it comes to leading God's way, we aren't to emulate the world's version of success. In fact, Jesus said the world's leaders lord it over their followers, but "Not so with you."

Instead of puffing ourselves up and flexing our muscles, we are called by Jesus to lead by serving. He went on to model this style of leadership by washing His disciples' feet, which was a radical statement then and still is today.

What can you do if you are the elephant in the room? You can try something that I've found helpful: make yourself part of a committee where you are only one vote. For instance, we have a giving committee. There are seven people on it. I'm one vote. I can get outvoted. We've applied the same principle in the area of family employment. It's hard to be the elephant when you are only one vote.

You must decide. Do you want to tell people what to do and feel important, or do you want to serve and empower people and be important?

Have you ever worked under a leader who "lorded it over" you and others? What did that feel like? How did that style of leadership impact the organization? If you are leading a team, division, or department, have you identified an apprentice yet?

Disagree and Commit

Have confidence in your leaders and submit to their authority, because they keep watch over you as those who must
give an account. Do this so that their work will be a joy, not
a burden, for that would be of no benefit to you.

Hebrews 13:17

The leadership book *Great by Choice* describes Intel's recipe
for success, which includes the "practice of constructive con-
frontation." Their leaders encouraged employees to "argue and
debate regardless of rank, and then commit once a decision is
made—disagree and commit."*

Too often organizations get stuck, with their people either
avoiding difficult conversations because they fear conflict or
undermining decisions that get made because they disagree
with them. Both paths lead to stagnation and frustration.

In the church, we are instructed to submit to leadership
decisions in a way that is a joy to the leaders ultimately re-
sponsible for making those decisions. Does this mean we will

* Jim Collins and Morten T. Hansen, *Great by Choice: Uncertainty, Chaos,
and Luck—Why Some Thrive Despite Them All* (New York: Harper Business,
2011), 141.

agree with every decision they make? Of course not! But there is a way to disagree and still honor the leaders and support the decision, and that's what we are told to do in Hebrews 13.

These principles apply in the same way at Hobby Lobby. Sometimes we may face a decision where many disagree with me and feel uncomfortable with the direction I wish to take. But if I listen to them and fully hear them out and still believe my decision is best, I need for them to fully support the decision—to disagree and commit. But I have to be careful. Because I'm the leader, I can use my position or authority to force agreement. If I force agreement, I'll get people who say they agree, but their heart isn't in it. Over the long term, that's dangerous.

The opposite is also true. I may need to be the one to disagree and commit. My goal is to hire people smarter than me in their area and trust them to do their job. They may have a preferred course of action, and if we talk openly about it, I still need to let them make the decision. I need to disagree and commit as well.

Supporting those you disagree with is necessary, whether they are coworkers or family; it's one of those essential aspects of good leadership. It's worth repeating: disagree and commit.

———

Does your organization have a "disagree and commit" culture? If not, what small steps can you take to have an honest conversation about this issue?

Don't Be a Hero

> The eye cannot say to the hand, "I don't need you!" And the head cannot say to the feet, "I don't need you!"
>
> 1 Corinthians 12:21

Do you remember that scene from *Superman* when the hero saves the day by stopping a train full of people speeding toward a head-on collision? We love watching heroes do their thing in the movies, but this doesn't work out as well in real life.

I've watched would-be heroes at many businesses make the same mistake over and over again, and the end result is usually the same—instead of stopping the train, they get flattened by it! If you're a leader who moves forward with ideas without getting people on board, you're going to fail.

As Christians, this shouldn't surprise us. In 1 Corinthians 12, the apostle Paul devotes the entire chapter to the working of the body. He emphasizes how the body needs all parts working together. One part cannot say, "I don't need you," to any other part. Paul goes further in verse 25 and says that the "parts should have equal concern for each other."

Why? We need one another. We learn from one another. We strengthen one another.

Perhaps you've heard the phrase "we come to Christ as individuals but we grow in community." While there is a time and place for individuals to lead and make decisions, if we find ourselves living and making decisions in isolation, we are likely in a danger zone.

Good leaders support their teams and work toward harmony, which means other people must have a say. And good leaders aren't conceited; they don't attempt to do it alone but rather understand the only path to success centers on the team.

I admit to having had some hero tendencies early in my career. But it didn't take long to see how damaging other would-be heroes could be to their teams. If I didn't like to see it in them, I had to admit when I did the same things and make some changes.

If you have hero tendencies, one change you can make today is simply to not make decisions in isolation. Invite others into dialogue, especially those who have a different perspective. Hold your early appraisals lightly until you've heard from the team and found some common ground. Trust me, you don't want to get flattened by that train.

—

Which hero tendencies do you recognize in your own leadership? How can you involve more of the right people in the important decisions?

Responsibility with Authority

> Then Jesus came to them and said, "All authority in heaven and on earth has been given to me. Therefore go and make disciples."
>
> Matthew 28:18–19

Is there anything more frustrating and disheartening than being given a responsibility without the necessary authority to get the job done? We've all been on both sides of this dilemma, no doubt.

Leaders tend to get in trouble when they want to unload a responsibility onto someone else but don't want to let go of control. On the one hand, the leader desperately needs people to step up and assume responsibility for important assignments. On the other hand, they don't fully trust people to do it the right way. (And usually "the right way" means "the way I would do it.")

Can you imagine how Jesus must have felt turning over His ministry to the disciples just before He returned to His Father? Jesus literally bled and died for the church, and then

He delegated the responsibility for leading His church to a team of people who lacked a seminary education and often argued about which of them was the greatest.

Jesus succeeded in this by not only giving responsibility but also delegating His authority. He had all authority, and He deputized His disciples by giving them enough of that authority and by empowering them through sending the Holy Spirit.

Did they still make mistakes? Of course. Did they do everything just like Jesus would have done it? Not a chance. Did they turn the world upside down with the gospel? Absolutely.

So, if you want to lift your people to truly amazing heights of growth and effectiveness, lead like Jesus. Give authority commensurate with responsibility. Empower others by providing whatever they need to do the work. And always remember to model for them whatever you are asking them to do. Jesus didn't just give orders to be followed. He first showed His disciples exactly what servant leadership looked like and then challenged them to do likewise.

In what ways have you struggled with giving responsibility with authority? Have you ever had a boss who did this well? What did you learn from their example?

Your One Thing

Brothers and sisters, I do not consider myself yet to have taken hold of it. But one thing I do: Forgetting what is behind and straining toward what is ahead, I press on toward the goal to win the prize for which God has called me heavenward in Christ Jesus.

Philippians 3:13–14

God gave me one talent, not five. I buy and sell merchandise; that's my one thing. So often leaders feel like they have to be good at many things—or worse yet, everything. We've all seen what happens to people who try to do too much. It's hard to watch.

The apostle Paul focused on his one thing. When he was saved, God spoke through the prophet Ananias, "This man is my chosen instrument to proclaim my name to the Gentiles and their kings and to the people of Israel" (Acts 9:15). In fact, Paul often referred to himself as "the apostle to the Gentiles." Paul's one thing was to make Christ known among the Gentiles and establish faith communities that would literally spread the gospel to the ends of the earth.

Paul did many different things, but they all revolved around and related to his one thing. Not only did his single-minded devotion to his one thing give him focus but we read in Philippians 3 it also gave him the ability to leave the past behind and press on toward the prize that awaited him in heaven—hearing from God, "Well done, My good and faithful servant."

What's your one thing? Do you have organizational gifts? Are you really good at making people feel heard and cared for? Can you fix or build things with your hands? It's up to each of us to discover what our one thing is, and then to focus our time and attention on employing and developing that talent.

This discovery process may take a while, and that's okay. Moses was eighty before he discovered his one thing, but God used the last forty years of his life in a remarkable way that altered the course of history. He found his one thing, and that changed everything.

If you are still discovering your one thing, pay attention to what gives you joy and energy, what feels natural to you, and what God blesses so that you can bless others. What do you notice?

Diligence before Distinction

Do you see someone skilled in their work? They will serve before kings; they will not serve before officials of low rank.

Proverbs 22:29

I read recently that in 2022 Ford Motor Company sold 4.2 million vehicles worldwide, generating $158 billion in revenue.* Those numbers distinguish Ford as one of the oldest and most profitable companies in the world. But it didn't start that way.

In 1891, engineer Henry Ford began tinkering with an idea for a horseless carriage in his spare time. Working alone at night and on weekends, he kept honing his invention (which he called the "quadricycle") for over twelve years. There were no interviews, no TED Talks, and certainly no fame or fortune. He just kept at it. He believed in his idea and was willing to put in the long hours to bring it to life. Henry Ford is a per-

---

* Carlier, "Wholesale Vehicle Sales of the Ford Motor Company 2009–2022," Statista, March 17, 2023, https://www.statista.com/statistics/297315/ford-vehicle-sales/.

fect example of "diligence before distinction," and in 1903 he started Ford Motor Company.

People who are diligent enough to become skilled in their work will have opportunities and be recognized by those who can appreciate what they've done, according to Proverbs 22:29. But diligence must come first, and that's the hard part.

If you want the distinction that accompanies people who have excelled in their field and honed their craft, you must embrace diligent and sustained effort. Surely 99.9 percent of successful people had to "pay their dues" early on. Most experienced setbacks and frustrations and made some big mistakes along the way. Success most often is made in a slow cooker, not a microwave.

And, like Henry Ford discovered, few people will pay you to get better at your craft. He learned how to build an automobile on his own time. He didn't quit his day job. This sort of work ethic flies in the face of current cultural pressures pushing us toward easy credit and overnight success. But in the end, even most of those dot-com millionaires were reminded that there is no shortcut when it comes to diligence and perseverance.

What stirs your heart so much that you would be willing to sacrifice comfort and immediate gratification to pursue it? Who can you share this with this week? How is God speaking to you about this?

Work as Worship

The Lord God took the man and put him in the Garden of Eden to work it and take care of it.

Genesis 2:15

In his 1928 bluegrass song "Big Rock Candy Mountain," Harry McClintock describes his vision of heaven on earth. One of his closing lyrics rejoices because "they hung the jerk that invented work."

I don't know about you, but there've been days I can relate to that sentiment! We all have struggles, frustrations, and setbacks in our work. The Bible says that because of sin we will work by the sweat of our brow and fight against thorns and thistles that constantly impede our progress. But before we embrace the idea of hanging the jerk who invented work, we need to remember that work was God's idea.

In Genesis 2, before Adam and Eve rebelled against God, they were placed in the Garden of Eden to *work* it and take care of it. Work, as it turns out, was not a result of the fall but a gift given to humankind created in the image of God that affords dignity and purpose.

God could have done all the work Himself and just let Adam and Eve lounge around all day, but He didn't. Why not? Because, according to Jesus in John 5:17, God is always at work. Since we are created in God's image, we are called to work, to create, to build, and to care for God's creation.

It's no wonder Paul told the Thessalonians that if someone was unwilling to work, they shouldn't eat. Not only was this an admonition against laziness but more so it was an appeal to grow up as image bearers of God.

Wise parents require their children to do appropriate work according to their ability; they don't do their work for them and rob them of dignity. Wise employers require their employees to work and give them the tools and resources to do their jobs effectively. Your work is an important part of your worship, so do it with all your heart.

—

How does viewing work as part of your worship impact the way you think about your job? If you are a parent, what could you do to empower your children to be more successful in their work?

DAY 90

God's Handiwork

> For we are God's handiwork, created in Christ Jesus to do good works, which God prepared in advance for us to do.
>
> Ephesians 2:10

As I mentioned earlier, Hobby Lobby began in our garage with a little handiwork. Our family cut pieces of wood and glued them together to make small picture frames. We worked with our hands to create something of value. These frames would hold pictures painted by their owners, who proudly hung them in their homes, displaying their handiwork.

There is a special satisfaction people feel when they build or create something with their hands and then step back to view it after it's finished. God feels that kind of satisfaction when He looks at His handiwork: you and me. Of course, none of us are finished works of art just yet, but we are in process. And that process speaks to what God is creating in and through our lives; we are created in Christ Jesus to do good works, according to Ephesians 2.

But it gets even better! You aren't created in Christ Jesus to do just any good work but those specific good works God prepared in advance for *you* to do. Think about that for a moment. God prepared good works for you to do before you were even born. God designed you, He gifted you, and He gave you a certain personality so that you could do something special with your life—something no one else who ever lived could do exactly like you. In a very real way you are God's handiwork, His masterpiece.

Here are four questions you can ask yourself to help discern what kind of good works God has prepared for you to do.

1. What am I interested in and what gets me excited?
2. What brings me joy and a deep sense of satisfaction?
3. What breaks my heart and what do I find myself complaining about?
4. What needs do I notice in my day-to-day activities?

—

As you reflect on your responses, what patterns do you notice? Share your answers with a trusted person who knows you well, and ask for their input. What do they see in you?

DAVID GREEN borrowed $600 in 1970 to start making picture frames in a garage. He is now CEO of Hobby Lobby, which employs fifty thousand people at almost one thousand stores in forty-eight states and grosses $8 billion a year. The coauthor of *Giving It All Away . . . and Getting It All Back Again*, Green received the World Changer Award in 2013 and is a past recipient of the Ernst & Young Entrepreneur of the Year Award. David and his wife, Barbara, are the proud parents of three, grandparents of ten, and great-grandparents of seventeen (and counting). They live in Oklahoma City.

BILL HIGH is well known for three core values: family, legacy, and generosity. After practicing law with a large law firm in Kansas City, he started what became one of the largest Christian foundations in the country. He began working with the Green family more than twenty years ago. He began consulting with families on generational legacy through his company 7 Generation Legacy. He's led family legacy workshops across the country and he also serves as the Chief Family Officer of Legacy Stone, a ministry to help families succeed today and for generations to come.